Listen and Learn German

GUSTAVE MATHIEU

Chairman, Dept. of Foreign Languages & Literatures, California State College at Fullerton

GUY STERN

Chairman, Dept. of Germanic Languages & Literatures, University of Cincinnati

and the Editorial Staff of
DOVER PUBLICATIONS, INC.

DOVER PUBLICATIONS, INC.

NEW YORK

THE GERMAN ALPHABET (not recorded)

The German alphabet is given below along with the pronunciation of each letter according to the transcription used in the manual. You will find it useful in spelling out names and addresses. The Gothic type face is also given although it is gradually disappearing from usage. Most books and newspapers, and all road signs and public notices are printed in the Roman face.

Gothic Face	*Roman Face*	*Pronunciation of German letter*
𝔄𝔞	Aa	ah
𝔅𝔟	Bb	bay
ℭ𝔠	Cc	tsay
𝔇𝔡	Dd	day
𝔈𝔢	Ee	ay
𝔉𝔣	Ff	ef
𝔊𝔤	Gg	gay
ℌ𝔥	Hh	hah
ℑ𝔦	Ii	ee
𝔍𝔧	Jj	yawt
𝔎𝔨	Kk	kah
𝔏𝔩	Ll	el
𝔐𝔪	Mm	em
𝔑𝔫	Nn	en
𝔒𝔬	Oo	oh
𝔓𝔭	Pp	pay
𝔔𝔮	Qq	koo
ℜ𝔯	Rr	ehr
𝔖ſ, 𝔰	Ss	es
𝔗𝔱	Tt	tay
𝔘𝔲	Uu	oo
𝔙𝔳	Vv	fow
𝔚𝔴	Ww	vay
𝔛𝔵	Xx	iks
𝔜𝔶	Yy	EWP-see-lawn
ℨ𝔷	Zz	tset

Manufactured in the United States of America

International Standard Book Number: 0-486-20878-8

Library of Congress Catalog Card Number: R60-106

CONTENTS

INTRODUCTION

The Plan and Presentation of "Listen and Learn"

Listen and Learn German is an introductory course designed to give you the basic sentences, phrases, and vocabulary that you will need in almost every travel situation. The course does not pretend to teach the grammatical structure of German through a series of graded lessons. You will, however, absorb much of the structure of German in the same unconscious way in which you first learned English as a child. You need not start at the beginning; *Listen and Learn* whatever sections interest you. Although a systematic study is probably most desirable, don't feel obliged to master any one series of phrases before going on to the next. This course differs from many others in that whatever you learn will be useful, regardless of the amount of previous study or your ability to retain.

You will observe that *Listen and Learn German* is a straightforward course, designed to help you solve real travel problems. Its value rests as much in what is omitted as in what is included. You will learn how to ask for small change (an urgent need in travel), but do not expect to find "This is the pen of my aunt."

Listen and Learn German teaches you principally what *you* will say. This plan is a deliberate editorial policy based on travel experience. No editor could possibly anticipate the exact form in which your questions will be answered. A waiter may be anything from taciturn to over-talkative, and may answer your question by a silent nod or with voluble news of his cousin in Cleveland. The editors have therefore framed most of the questions and statements to elicit a simple response that will probably contain the very words in your question.

The section on making yourself understood (entries 47 to 61) will also aid you in understanding others. Phrases such as "Please speak more slowly," and "Does anyone here speak English?" are essential because the correct pronunciation you will achieve through imitation will often suggest to your listener a greater mastery of the language than you may actually have.

Suggested Method for Study—The Records

In the recordings, each item is spoken in English and in German, followed by a pause sufficiently long to allow for repetition.* If you are completely unfamiliar with German, the pause may seem short at first, but you will find that as you become more familiar with each entry, the pause will be adequate for repetition. After some practice, you may wish to use this pause to anticipate the next item and check your pronunciation against that of the speaker. If at first you listen to the records while following the text, you will later find the separate study of the record and text more meaningful. Play the records whenever you have an opportunity, while working, engaging in a hobby—whenever you are within listening range of a record player. Although active participation is best, even passive but repeated listening will familiarize you with useful German.

* Except for four brief sections of dialogue delivered at the normal rate of speed in order to acquaint you with the rhythm and flow of German in ordinary conversation. In the recordings, each such section begins with a reminder that dialogue follows.

Suggested Method for Study—The Manual

The *Listen and Learn German* manual is complete in itself and is designed so that you can carry it in your pocket for reference and study. Read it at odd moments—while commuting, eating, waiting—and try to learn 10 or 15 phrases a day, testing your pronunciation against the records later. In 30 to 60 days, you will know what is essential for travel.

Be sure to take the manual with you when you go abroad. All that you have learned will be available to you for reference and refresher study. You will find the extensive topic and word index on pages 121-130 especially helpful. Notice that each entry in the book is numbered and that the index refers to these numbers. This enables you to locate the information you need quickly, without having to search the entire page.

Use the index to test yourself. It contains every important word and phrase that you have learned in *Listen and Learn German.* Test your vocabulary and your ability to form phrases and questions from the words in the index.

The manual is designed to help you form additional sentences of your own. For the words in square brackets you can substitute the words immediately following (in the same sentence or in the indented entries below). For example, the entry

I am [hungry] thirsty.

provides two sentences: "I am hungry" and "I am thirsty." Three sentences are provided by the entry

I am a [student].
—— teacher.
—— business man.

As your German vocabulary increases, you will find that you can express a wide range of thoughts by the proper substitution of words in these model sentences.

Speak German When You Travel

When you travel in Germany, Austria, or Switzerland, do not be timid about using what you have learned. The native listener is always pleased and flattered when you attempt to speak his language. Whether this is your first trip or you twenty-first, your native listener will know that you are an American (years of intensive study will never disguise this fact), and he is ready to accept pronunciation and grammar less than perfect. So do not be self-conscious if your speech is halting and awkward. Speak politely, boldly, and clearly. Timid mumbling may be a greater barrier to comprehension than faulty ü's and ö's. Remember that your purpose is to communicate, not to pass as a person whose native tongue is German.

Listen and Learn German will enable you to communicate on a simple but very practical level. You will make yourself understood on everyday matters. With time and practice, improvement will come and the range of your conversation will expand. Do not, however, let your present inability to discuss German music or politics inhibit you in asking questions in German. You know your own language limitations, and you must speak German within and in spite of them.

Bear in mind that your native listener is not judging or grading you. He is kindly disposed towards you and is especially interested in trying to communicate. When you succeed in making yourself understood in

German, you will have achieved your aim. If you are interested in a grade, score yourself 100%.

Speak the German you have learned from *Listen and Learn German*. The effort will not only make your travel more exciting and rewarding, but will also contribute to better foreign relations. Many Americans go abroad expecting all peoples of the world to speak English—an attitude that non-Americans find narrow. If you are willing to meet and speak with people in their own language, you may not impress them with your command of the subjunctive, but you will create an impression more representative of the warmth and democratic feeling of America. This impression may be more valuable than thousands of words of propaganda.

FOR FURTHER STUDY

After you have mastered the material of *Listen and Learn German,* you may wish to continue with more formal study in order to become more fluent in speaking, reading, and writing. It is possible to carry on study by yourself with a few well-selected books and with such audio-visual aids as German movies, newspapers, records, etc.

The following books can be purchased through your local dealer at the publisher's current (1974) list price.

Dictionaries

Langenscheidt's New Pocket German Dictionary: German-English, English-German, Hippocrene Books, Inc., 171 Madison Avenue, New York, N.Y. 10016. $3.50.

Pocket Oxford German Dictionary (German-English, English-German), M. L. Barker and H. Homeyer, Oxford University Press, 200 Madison Avenue, New York, N.Y. 10016. $5.95.

Cassell's German-English, English-German Dictionary, Funk & Wagnalls Publishing Company, 666 Fifth Avenue, New York, N.Y. 10019. $8.95.

Introductory Grammars

Basic German: An Introduction, by Herbert Lederer, Charles Scribner's Sons, 597 Fifth Avenue, New York, N.Y. 10017. $3.95.

Basic Spoken German Grammar, by E. J. Allen Pfeffer and others, Prentice-Hall, Inc., Englewood Cliffs, N.J. 07632. $9.95.

For Self-Study

Colloquial German, by P. F. Doring, Dover Publications, Inc., 180 Varick Street, New York, N.Y. 10014. $2.75.

German: How to Speak and Write It, by Joseph Rosenberg, Dover Publications, Inc., 180 Varick Street, New York, N.Y. 10014. $2.75.

Review Grammar

If you studied German in high-school or college you might find the following review grammar useful.

Essential German Grammar, by G. Stern and E. F. Bleiler, Dover Publications, Inc., 180 Varick Street, New York, N.Y. 10014. $1.25.

Readers

The following readers make a good companion study to your beginning and review grammar.

Cultural Graded Readers, C. R. Goedsche and W. E. Glättli, 5 paperback volumes, Van Nostrand-Reinhold Company, 450 West 33rd Street, New York, N.Y. 10001. $1.25 per volume.

The following publishers have an extensive list of foreign language books and will supply their catalogues upon request:

Ginn & Company, 191 Spring Street, Lexington, Mass. 02173

D. C. Heath & Company, 125 Spring Street, Lexington, Mass. 02173

Oxford University Press, Inc., 200 Madison Avenue, New York, N.Y. 10016

Houghton-Mifflin Company, 2 Park Street, Boston, Mass. 02107

Holt, Rinehart and Winston, Inc., 383 Madison Avenue, New York, N.Y. 10017

American Book Company, 450 West 33rd Street, New York, N.Y. 10001.

German Periodicals

To develop your comprehension, the following publications are recommended. Of course, they require a more advanced grasp of German, and you would do well first to buy an individual copy to determine whether or not it is within your reading ability.

Aufbau, 2121 Broadway, New York, N.Y. 10023. Weekly. 50¢ per copy; $17.00 for one year.

Das Beste, Reader's Digest, Pleasantville, N.Y. 10570. The German edition of the *Reader's Digest* is published monthly. 50¢ per copy; $4.97 for one year. (It takes about three months for a subscription to become effective.)

General Literature

Your local dealer probably has a small selection of foreign language books, but a visit there may be rewarding. The following specialist dealers have larger stocks ranging from elementary to advanced levels. Some will send you catalogues and announcements if you drop them a card.

Kroch's & Brentano's, 29 South Wabash Avenue, Chicago, Ill. 60603

R. H. Macy's Book Department, Herald Square, New York, N.Y. 10001

Adler's Foreign Books, 162 Fifth Avenue, New York, N.Y. 10010

Barnes and Noble, Inc., 105 Fifth Avenue, New York, N.Y. 10003

Brentano's Inc., 586 Fifth Avenue, New York, N.Y. 10036

Central Book Store, 174 Michigan Avenue, Chicago, Ill. 60601

Schoenhof's Foreign Books, Inc., 1280 Massachusetts Avenue, Cambridge, Mass. 02138

Stechert-Hafner, Inc., 866 Third Avenue, New York, N.Y. 10022

Henry Mielke Company, 242 East 86th Street, New York, N.Y. 10028.

Recordings

After you have mastered the basic difficulties of comprehension, you will enjoy listening to some of the interesting works of German literature, as recorded by leading German actors and actresses. A look through the *Schwann Guide* (available at most record shops) will give you a good idea of what works are available.

Many German recordings can be purchased from Henry Mielke Company, 242 East 86th Street, New York, N.Y. 10028.

German Radio Programs

Broadcasts in German provide a variety of intonation, expression, and subject matter, and thus offer an excellent means of quickening your comprehension. German-language programs are offered by more than 80 stations in the United States. Your local paper is the best source of current information.

PRONUNCIATION

A simplified phonetic transcription is given as an aid to correct pronunciation. The transcription should be read as though it were English, with special attention to those sounds, marked with arrows in the table, which have no English equivalents. Stressed syllables are printed in capital letters. The rules of German pronunciation are not difficult, and their application is regular. **It is not necessary to memorize these rules in order to benefit from the records.** The best guide is listening to native speakers and attempting careful imitation. In our phonetic system consistency is sometimes sacrificed for simplicity and ease of comprehension. You are urged to use it only as a temporary guide.

Note on Vowels

Vowel sounds in German, as in most foreign languages, usually present the greatest problem, not only to the beginner, but also to the advanced student. Foreign accents that persist in fluent speakers of English, French, German, and other languages are usually caused by slight distortions of vowel sounds. The following notes on pronunciation are to direct your listening and perhaps make your ear more critical to the subtle differences between German and English (but bear in mind that mastery or study of these differences is not essential. You will achieve comprehension by simple imitation of the speaker).

In German as in English, there are *long* and *short*

vowel sounds. As a general rule vowels are long when followed by a single consonant and short when followed by two or more consonants. The following examples will serve to illustrate:

Long *a*, as in *father*	Short *a*, like *u* in *sun*
kam (came)	*Kammer* (chamber, room)
Long *e*, like *ay* in *day*	Short *e*, as in *met*
wen (whom)	*wenn* (when, if)
Long *i*, like *ee* in *feel*	Short *i*, as in *still*
Stil (style)	*still* (quiet)
Long *o*, as in *stove*	Short *o*, like *aw* in *lawyer*
Ofen (stove)	*offen* (open)
Long *u*, like *oo* in *food*	Short *u*, like *oo* in *foot*
Mut (courage)	*Mutter* (mother)

There are a few exceptions among common, one-syllable words such as *von*, *man*, and *mit*, to which the phonetic transcription will serve as a guide. German vowels are always long when followed by *h*, or when doubled.

The vowels *ö* and *ü*, as well as the consonants *r* and *ch*, are sounds which have no English equivalents. They have been marked with an arrow in the table because more attention should be paid to these sounds.

The authors have introduced these remarks on phonetic differences with considerable hesitancy, for fear that they might hinder speaking by the beginner, but to readers who have studied German before, or are familiar with other foreign languages, these remarks will be more comprehensible and useful. The beginner should consider this material on pronunciation as hints for improvement, rather than essential material which must be mastered before he begins to speak.

SCHEME OF PRONUNCIATION

Letter	*Transcription*	*Example*	*Notes*
a	ah	as in f*a*ther	The short *a* is like the long, except in duration. It more nearly resembles the *u* in such words as s*u*n, h*u*nt, etc.
b	b	as in *b*oy	At the end of a word, *b* is pronounced *p*.
c	ts, k		*c* rarely occurs alone, except in words of foreign origin. For the pronunciation of *c* in the combinations *sch*, *ck*, and *ch*, see p. 22.
d	d	as in *d*ay.	At the end of a word, *d* is pronounced *t*.
e	ay (long)	as in d*ay*time	A pure vowel and not a diphthong as in English, where *ay* is actually composed of two sounds: eh-ee.
e	e or eh (short)	as in m*e*t	
e	e (mute) uh		At the end of a word, *e* is a neutral vowel as in th*e* boy.
f	f	as in *f*all	

Letter	*Transcription*	*Example*	*Notes*
g	g	as in *g*o	In a few words of French origin, the *g* is soft as in massa*g*e. It is never like the English *g* of *g*em.
h	h	as in *h*old	The *h* is silent after a vowel.
i	ee (long)	as in f*ee*l	
i	i or ih (short)	as in f*i*t	
j	y	as in *y*es	
k	k	as in *k*ite	
l	l	as in *l*ive	
m	m	as in *m*et	
n	n	as in *n*et	
o	o or oh (long)	as in ph*oto*	A pure vowel in German; not a diphthong as in English. The long *o* in English consists of two sounds: oh-oo. Try the long oh without ending on the sound of oo.

Letter	*Transcription*	*Example*	*Notes*
o	aw (short)	as in l*aw*yer	When a short *o* is followed by *r*, it has been transcribed as o. The German word *fort* is pronounced like the English word *fort*.
p	p	as in *p*et	
qu	kv	as in la*ck* *v*ariety	
➔r	r	as in *r*ise	The *r* may either be trilled with the tip of the tongue as is done in Spanish or Italian, or produced by vibrating the uvula against the back of the tongue, like the sound you make when you gargle.
s	s, z, sh	as in *s*ee, *z*eal, *sh*ell	Pronounced like z at the beginning of a word or between two vowels. Pronounced sh in the combinations *st* and *sp* when they occur at the beginning of a word or syllable. Elsewhere, or when doubled, it is pronounced as in *s*ee.
t	t	as in *t*ake	

Letter	Tran-scription	Example	Notes
u	oo (long)	as in f*oo*d	
u	o͝o (short)	as in f*oo*t	
v	f	as in *f*it	
w	v	as in *v*ase	
x	ks	as in loo*ks*	
y	varies		Occurs only in foreign words and is usually pronounced as in the foreign language or like the letter *ü*.
z	ts	as in le*ts*	
ä	ay (long)	as in d*ay*time	(See note on long *e*, p. 18
ä	e or eh (short)	as in m*e*t	
➜ö	e̅r	as in h*er*	Do not pronounce the *r* itself. If you pronounce the words *purr*, *girl*, *demur* as is done in England and some parts of the eastern United States, you will have a good approximation of the sound. It may be long or short.
➜ü	ew	as in f*ew*	Like the French word *rue*. Round the lips as if to say oo, and without changing the position of the lips, say ee.

Letter	*Tran-scription*	*Example*	*Notes*
➔ch	kh (guttural)	no English equivalent; *ch* as in Scotch word lo*ch*	*ch* is a guttural sound after *a*, *o*, and *u*; palatal after all other vowels and consonants.
➔ch	$\overline{\text{sh}}$ (palatal)	no English equivalent	You will be understood if you say *sh* as in *sh*ell, or an exaggerated *h* as in *h*ue. Try to pronounce the word *shell* with the tip of the tongue against the lower gums.
chs	ks	as in loo*ks*	
ck	k	as in ba*ck*	
ng	ng	as in si*ng*er, never as in hu*ng*er	
sch	sh	as in *sh*ell	

DIPHTHONGS

ai, ei	i	as in k*i*te
au	ow	as in c*ow*, never as in l*ow*
äu, eu	oy	as in b*oy*

SOCIAL CONVERSATION

SIDE ONE, BAND I

1. Good morning.
Guten Morgen.
GOO-ten MOR-gen.

2. Good evening.
Guten Abend.
GOO-ten AH-bent.

3. Hello.
Guten Tag.
GOO-ten tahk.

4. Good-bye.
Auf Wiedersehen.
owf VEE-der-zay-en.

5. I wish to make an appointment with Mr. Braun.
Ich möchte eine Verabredung mit Herrn Braun treffen.
ish MERSH-tuh I-nuh fehr-AHP-ray-doong mit hehrn brown TREF-fen.

6. May I introduce [Mr., Mrs.] Miss Müller?
Darf ich [Herrn, Frau] Fräulein Müller vorstellen?
dahrf ish [hehrn, frow] FROY-lin MEWL-ler FOR-shtel-len?

7. —— My wife.
Meine Frau.
MI-nuh frow.

8. —— My husband.
Mein Mann.
min mahn.

9. —— **My daughter.**
Meine Tochter.
MĪ-nuh TAWKH-ter.

10. —— **My son.**
Mein Sohn.
mīn zohn.

11. —— **My sister.**
Meine Schwester.
MĪ-nuh SHVES-ter.

12. —— **My brother.**
Mein Bruder.
mīn BROO-der.

13. —— **My child.**
Mein Kind.
mīn kint.

14. —— **My friend.**
Mein Freund (*masc.*).
mīn froynt.

15. **I am glad to meet you.**
Sehr angenehm.
zehr AHN-geh-naym.

16. **How are you?**
Wie geht es Ihnen?
vee gayt es EE-nen?

17. **Fine, thanks, and you?**
Gut, danke, und Ihnen?
goot, DAHNG-kuh, oont EE-nen?

18. **How are things?**
Was gibt's sonst?
vahs gipts zawnst?

19. So, so.
Es geht so.
es gayt zo.

20. All right.
Gut.
goot.

21. How is your family?
Wie geht es Ihrer Familie?
vee gayt es EE-rer fah-MEEL-yuh?

22. Please sit down.
Bitte nehmen Sie Platz.
BIT-tuh NAY-men zee plahts.

23. I had a very nice time.
Es war sehr nett.
es vahr zehr net.

24. Give my regards to your aunt and uncle.
Grüssen Sie Ihre Tante und Ihren Onkel von mir.
GREW-sen zee EE-ruh TAHN-tuh oont EE-ren AWNG-kel fun meer.

25. Come to see us.
Besuchen Sie uns.
beh-ZOO-khen zee oons.

26. May I call on you again?
Darf ich Sie wieder besuchen?
dahrf ish zee VEE-der beh-ZOO-khen?

27. I like you very much.
Ich habe Sie sehr gern.
ish HAH-buh zee zehr gehrn.

28. Congratulations!
Herzliche Glückwünsche!
HEHRTS-lih-shuh GLEWK-vewn-shuh!

29. Happy Birthday!
Herzlichen Geburtstag!
HEHRTS-lih-shen geh-BOORTS-tahk!

30. Happy New Year!
Glückliches Neujahr!
GLEWK-lih-shes NOY-yahr!

31. Merry Christmas!
Fröhliche Weihnachten!
FRER-lih-shuh VI-nahkh-ten!

YOURSELF

SIDE ONE, BAND 2

32. My name is John.
Ich heisse Johann.
ish HI-suh YO-hahn.

33. I am an American citizen.
Ich bin Bürger der Vereinigten Staaten.
ish bin BEWR-ger dehr fehr-I-nish-ten SHTAH-ten.

34. My mailing address is Hotel Adler, Berlin.
Meine Postadresse ist Hotel Adler, Berlin.
MI-nuh PAWST-ah-dres-suh ist ho-TEL AHT-ler, behr-LEEN.

35. I am a [student.]
Ich bin [Student].*
ish bin shtoo-DENT.

36. —— teacher.
Lehrer.*
LAY-rer.

37. —— business man.
Geschäftsmann.
geh-SHEFTS-mahn.

* The feminine forms of *Student* and *Lehrer* are *Studentin* and *Lehrerin*.

38. I am a friend of Frank's.
Ich bin ein Freund von Franz.*
ish̄ bin īn froynt fun frahnts.

39. I am here on vacation.
Ich mache eine Ferienreise.
ish̄ MAH-khuh Ī-nuh FEHR-yen-rī-zuh.

40. I am here on a business trip.
Ich mache eine Geschäftsreise.
ish̄ MAH-khuh Ī-nuh geh-SHEFTS-rī-zuh.

41. I am traveling to Berlin.
Ich reise nach Berlin.
ish̄ RĪ-zuh nahkh behr-LEEN.

42. I am [warm] cold.
Mir ist [warm] kalt.
meer ist [vahrm] kahlt.

43. I am [hungry] thirsty.
Ich habe [Hunger] Durst.
ish̄ HAH-buh [HOŎNG-er] doŏrst.

44. I am [busy] tired.
Ich bin [beschäftigt] müde.
ish̄ bin [beh-SHEF-tish̄t] MEW-duh.

45. I am [glad] sorry.†
Ich bin [froh] traurig.
ish̄ bin [fro] TROW-rish̄.

46. I am in a hurry.
Ich habe es eilig.
ish̄ HAH-buh es Ī-lish̄.

* A woman would say *Ich bin eine Freundin von Franz.*

† The more usual expression for "I am sorry" is Es tut mir leid (*es toot meer līt*).

MAKING YOURSELF UNDERSTOOD

47. Do you speak English?
Sprechen Sie Englisch?
SHPREH-shen zee ENG-lish?

48. Does anyone here speak English?
Spricht hier jemand Englisch?
shprisht heer YAY-mahnt ENG-lish?

49. I speak only English.
Ich spreche nur Englisch.
ish SHPREH-shuh noor ENG-lish.

50. I can read a little German.
Ich kann ein bisschen Deutsch lesen.
ish kahn in BIS-shen doytsh LAY-zen.

51. Please speak more slowly.
Bitte, sprechen Sie langsamer.
BIT-tuh, SHPREH-shen zee LAHNG-zah-mer.

52. I (do not) understand.
Ich verstehe (nicht).
ish fehr-SHTAY-uh (nisht).

53. Do you understand me?
Verstehen Sie mich?
fehr-SHTAY-en zee mish?

54. I (do not) know.
Ich weiss (nicht).
ish vis (nisht).

55. I (do not) think so.
Ich glaube (nicht).
ish GLOW-buh (nisht).

56. Repeat it, please.
Wiederholen Sie es, bitte.
vee-der-HO-len zee es, BIT-tuh.

57. Write it down, please.
Schreiben Sie es, bitte.
SHRĪ-ben zee es, BIT-tuh.

58. What does this word mean?
Was bedeutet dieses Wort?
vahs beh-DOY-tet DEE-zes vort?

59. What is that?
Was ist das?
vahs ist dahs?

60. How do you say "pencil" in German?
Wie sagt man „pencil" auf Deutsch?
vee zahkt mahn "pencil" owf doytsh?

61. How do you spell "Heidelberg"?
Wie buchstabiert man „Heidelberg"?
vee bookh-shtah-BEERT mahn "HĪ-del-behrk"?

USEFUL WORDS AND EXPRESSIONS

SIDE ONE, BAND 3

62. Yes.
Ja.
yah.

63. No.
Nein.
nīn.

64. Perhaps.
Vielleicht.
fee-LĪSHT.

65. Please.
Bitte.
BIT-tuh.

66. Excuse me.
Entschuldigen Sie.
ent-SHOOL-dih-gen zee.

67. Thanks (very much).
Danke (sehr).
DAHNG-kuh (zayr).

68. You are welcome.
Bitte.
BIT-tuh.

69. It is all right.
Es ist gut.
es ist goot.

70. It doesn't matter.
Das macht nichts.
dahs mahkht nishts.

71. That is all.
Das ist alles.
dahs ist AHL-les.

72. Who are you, please?
Wer sind Sie, bitte?
vehr zint zee, BIT-tuh?

73. Who is [that boy]?
Wer is [der Junge] dort?
vehr ist [dehr YOONG-uh] dawrt?

74. —— that girl
das Mädchen.
dahs MAYD-shen.

75. —— that man.
der Herr.
dehr hehr.

76. —— that woman.
die Dame.
dee DAH-muh.

77. Where is [the men's room]?
Wo ist [die Herrentoilette].
vo ist [dee Hehr-ren-toh-ah-LET-tuh]?

78. —— the ladies' room.
die Damentoilette.
dee DAH-men-toh-ah-LET-tuh.

79. Who?
Wer?
vehr?

80. Why?
Warum?
vah-ROOM?

81. How?
Wie?
vee?

82. What do you wish?
Was wünschen Sie?
vahs VEWN-shen zee?

83. Come here!
Kommen Sie her!
KAWM-men zee HEHR!

84. Come in!
Herein!
hehr-ĪN!

85. Wait a moment!
Warten Sie einen Augenblick!
VAHR-ten zee Ī-nen OW-gen-blick!

86. Listen!
Hören Sie zu!
HER-ren zee TSOO!

87. Look out!
Passen Sie auf!
PAHS-sen zee OWF!

88. Attention!
Achtung!
AHKH-toong!

DIFFICULTIES AND REPAIRS

89. Can you [help me] tell me?
Können Sie [mir helfen] mir sagen?
KĒR-nen zee [meer HEL-fen] meer ZAH-gen?

90. I am looking for my friends.
Ich suche meine Freunde.
ish ZOO-khuh MĪ-nuh FROYN-duh.

91. I cannot find my hotel address.
Ich kann meine Hoteladresse nicht finden.
ish kahn MĪ-nuh ho-TEL-ah-dres-suh nisht FIN-den.

92. She has lost [her handbag].
Sie hat [ihre Handtasche] verloren.
zee haht [EE-ruh HAHNT-tah-shuh] fehr-LO-ren.

93. —— her wallet.
ihr Portemonnaie.
eer port-mawn-NAY.

94. He forgot [his money].
Er hat [sein Geld] vergessen.
ehr haht [zīn gelt] fehr-GES-sen.

95. —— his keys.
seine Schlüssel.
ZĪ-nuh SHLEWS-sel.

96. They have missed their train.
Sie haben ihren Zug verpasst.
zee HAH-ben EE-ren tsook fehr-PAHST.

97. What am I to do?
Was soll ich tun?
vahs zawl ish̄ toon?

98. My glasses are broken.
Meine Brille ist zerbrochen.
MĪ-nuh BRIL-luh ist tsehr-BRAW-khen.

99. Can you repair these shoes?
Können Sie diese Schuhe reparieren?
KER̄-nen zee DEE-zuh SHOO-uh reh-pah-REE-ren?

100. The lost and found desk.
Das Fundbüro.
dahs FOONT-bew-ro.

101. The police station.
Das Polizeirevier.
dahs paw-lih-TSĪ-reh-veer.

102. I will call a policemen.
Ich werde einen Polizisten rufen.
ish̄ VEHR-duh Ī-nen paw-lih-TSIH-sten ROO-fen.

103. The American consulate.
Das amerikanische Konsulat.
dahs ah-may-ree-KAH-nish-uh kawn-zoo-LAHT.

CUSTOMS

SIDE ONE, BAND 4

104. Where is the customs?
Wo is der Zoll?
vo ist dehr tsawl?

105. Here is [my baggage].
Hier ist [mein Gepäck].
heer ist [mīn geh-PEK].

106. —— my passport.
mein Pass.
mīn pahs.

107. —— my identification papers.
mein Ausweis.
mīn OWS-vīs.

108. The bags to the right are mine.
Die Koffer rechts gehören mir.
dee KAWF-fer res̄h̄ts geh-HĒR̄-ren meer.

109. I have nothing to declare.
Ich habe nichts zu verzollen.
is̄h̄ HAH-buh nis̄h̄ts tsoo fehr-TSAWL-len.

110. All this is for my personal use.
All dies ist für meinen persönlichen Gebrauch.
ahl dees ist fewr MĪ-nen pehr-ZĒR̄N-lis̄h̄-en geh-BROWKH.

111. Must I open everything?
Muss ich alles öffnen?
moos is̄h̄ AHL-les ĒR̄F-nen?

112. I cannot open the trunk.
Ich kann den Koffer nicht öffnen.
is̄h̄ kahn dayn KAWF-fer nis̄h̄t ĒR̄F-nen.

113. There is nothing here but clothing.
Es sind nur Kleidungsstücke darin.
es zint noor KLĪ-doongs-shtew-kuh dah-RIN.

114. These are gifts.
Dies sind Geschenke.
dees zint geh-SHENG-kuh.

115. Are these things dutiable?
Sind diese Sachen zollpflichtig?
zint DEE-zuh ZAH-khen TSAWL-pflis̄h̄-tis̄h̄?

116. How much must I pay?
Wieviel muss ich bezahlen?
VEE-feel moos ish beh-TSAH-len?

117. This is all I have.
Dies ist alles, was ich habe.
dees ist AHL-les, vahs ish HAH-buh.

118. Have you finished?
Sind Sie fertig?
zint zee FEHR-tish?

BAGGAGE

119. Where can I check my baggage through to Berlin?
Wo kann ich mein Gepäck nach Berlin aufgeben?
vo kahn ish min geh-PEK nahkh behr-LEEN OWF-gay-ben?

120. The baggage room.
Der Gepäckraum.
dehr geh-PEK-rowm.

121. The baggage check.
Der Gepäckschein.
dehr geh-PEK-shin.

122. I want to leave these packages for a while.
Ich will diese Pakete eine Zeitlang hier lassen.
ish vil DEE-zuh pah-KAY-tuh Ī-nuh TSĪT-lahng heer LAHS-sen.

123. Handle this very carefully!
Fassen Sie dies sehr vorsichtig an!
FAHS-sen zee dees zehr FOR-sish-tish AHN!

124. Follow me.
Folgen Sie mir.
FAWL-gen zee meer.

125. Porter, put everything in a taxi.
Gepäckträger, bringen Sie bitte alles in ein Taxi.
geh-PEK-tray-ger, BRING-en zee BIT-tuh AHL-les in īn TAHK-see.

TRAVEL: GENERAL EXPRESSIONS

SIDE TWO, BAND I

126. I want to go [to the airline office].
Ich möchte [zum Büro der Fluglinie] gehen.
īsh MĒRSH-tuh [tsoom BEW-ro dehr FLOOK-leen-yuh] GAY-en.

127. —— to the travel agent's office.
zum Reisebüro.
tsoom RĪ-zuh-bew-ro.

128. —— to the tourist information office.
zum Auskunftsbüro.
tsoom OWS-koonfts-bew-ro.

129. —— to the hotel information office.
zum Zimmernachweis.
tsoom TSIM-mer-nahkh-vīs.

130. How long does the trip to Vienna take?
Wie lange dauert die Fahrt nach Wien?
vee LAHNG-uh DOW-ert dee fahrt nahkh veen?

131. When do we arrive in Munich?
Wann kommen wir in München an?
vahn KAWM-men veer in MEWN-shen AHN?

132. Is this the direct way to Zurich?
Ist dies der direkte Weg nach Zürich?
ist dees dehr dee-REK-tuh vayk nahkh TSEW-rish?

133. Please show me the way [to the business section].
Bitte zeigen Sie mir den Weg [zum Geschäftsviertel].
BIT-tuh TSĪ-gen zee meer dayn vayk [tsoom geh-SHEFTS-fihr-tel].

134. —— to the residential section.
zum Wohnviertel.
tsoom VOHN-feer-tel.

135. —— to the shopping section.
zum Einkaufszentrum.
tsoom ĪN-kowfs-tsen-troom.

136. —— to the city.
zu der Stadt.
tsoo dehr shtaht.

137. —— to the village.
zu dem Dorf.
tsoo daym dorf.

138. Do I turn [to the north]?
Muss ich [nach Norden] abbiegen?
moos ish [nahkh NOR-den] AHP-bee-gen?

139. —— to the south.
nach Süden.
nahkh ZEW-den.

140. —— to the east.
nach Osten.
nahkh AWS-ten.

141. —— **to the west.**
nach Westen.
nahkh VES-ten.

142. —— **to the right.**
nach rechts.
nahkh reshts.

143. —— **to the left.**
nach links.
nahkh links.

144. —— **at the traffic light.**
bei der Verkehrsampel.
bī dehr fehr-KAYRS-ahm-pel.

145. Where is it?
Wo ist es?
vo ist es?

146. Should I go [this way]? (*lit.*, **follow this street.**)
Soll ich [dieser Strasse] folgen?
zawl ish [DEE-zer SHTRAH-suh] FAWL-gen?

147. —— **that way.**
jener Strasse.
YAY-ner SHTRAH-suh.

148. Is it [on this side of the street]?
Ist es [auf dieser Seite der Strasse]?
ist es [owf DEE-zer ZĪ-tuh dehr SHTRAH-suh]?

149. —— **on the other side of the street.**
auf der anderen Seite der Strasse.
owf dehr AHN-deh-ren ZĪ-tuh dehr SHTRAH-suh?

150. —— **across the street.**
gegenüber.
gay-gen-EW-ber.

151. —— **at the corner.**
an der Ecke.
ahn der EK-kuh.

152. —— **in the middle.**
in der Mitte.
in dehr MIT-tuh.

153. —— **straight ahead.**
geradeaus.
geh-RAH-duh-ows.

154. —— **inside the station.**
im Bahnhof.
im BAHN-hohf.

155. —— **outside the lobby.**
ausserhalb der Halle.
OWS-ser-hahlb dehr HAHL-luh.

156. —— **opposite the park.**
gegenüber vom Park.
gay-gen-EW-ber fum pahrk.

157. —— **beside the school.**
neben der Schule.
NAY-ben dehr SHOO-luh.

158. —— **in front of the monument.**
vor dem Denkmal.
for daym DENK-mahl.

159. —— **behind the building.**
hinter dem Gebäude.
HIN-ter daym geh-BOY-duh.

160. Forward.
Vorwärts.
FOR-vehrts.

161. Back.
Zurück.
tsoo-REWK.

162. Do I have to cross the bridge?
Muss ich über die Brücke gehen?
moos ish EW-ber dee BREWK-kuh GAY-en?

163. How far is it?
Wie weit ist es?
vee vit ist es?

164. Is it near or far?
Ist es nah oder weit?
ist es nah O-der vit?

165. Can I walk there?
Kann ich dahin zu Fuss gehen?
kahn ish DAH-hin tsoo foos GAY-en?

166. Am I going in the right direction?
Gehe ich in der richtigen Richtung?
GAY-uh ish in dehr RISH-tih-gen RISH-toong?

167. What street is this?
Welche Strasse ist dies?
VEL-shuh SHTRAH-suh ist dees?

TICKETS

SIDE TWO, BAND 2

168. Where is the ticket office?
Wo ist der Fahrkartenschalter?
vo ist dehr FAHR-kahr-ten-shahl-ter?

169. How much is a round-trip ticket to Hamburg?
Wieviel kostet eine Fahrkarte nach Hamburg hin-und-zurück?
VEE-feel KAW-stet Ī-nuh FAHR-kahr-tuh nahkh HAHM-boorg hin-oont-tsoo-REWK?

170. A one-way ticket.
Eine einfache Fahrkarte.
Ī-nuh ĪN-fah-khuh FAHR-kahr-tuh.

171. First class.
Erste Klasse.
EHR-stuh KLAHS-suh.

172. Second class.
Zweite Klasse.
TSVĪ-tuh KLAHS-suh.

173. Local train.
Personenzug.
pehr-ZOH-nen-tsook.

174. Express train.
Schnellzug.
SHNEL-tsook.

175. A reserved seat.
Eine Platzkarte.
Ī-nuh PLAHTS-kahr-tuh.

176. The waiting room.
Der Warteraum.
dehr VAHR-tuh-rowm.

177. Can I stop at Frankfurt on the way?
Kann ich die Fahrt in Frankfurt unterbrechen?
kahn ish̄ dee fahrt in FRAHNK-foort oon-ter-BREH-sh̄en?

178. Can I get something to eat on the way?
Kann ich auf der Fahrt etwas zu essen bekommen?
kahn ish owf dehr fahrt ET-vahs tsoo ES-sen beh-KAWM-men?

BOAT

179. When must I go on board?
Wann muss ich an Bord gehen?
vahn moos ish ahn bort GAY-en?

180. Bon voyage!
Gute Reise!
GOO-tuh RĪ-zuh!

181. Where is [the purser]?
Wo ist [der Zahlmeister]?
vo ist [dehr TSAHL-mī-ster]?

182. —— the captain.
der Kapitän.
dehr kah-pee-TAYN.

183. The deck.
Das Deck.
dahs dek.

184. The deck chair.
Der Liegestuhl.
dehr LEE-guh-shtool.

185. The cabin.
Die Kabine.
dee kah-BEE-nuh.

186. I am seasick.
Ich bin seekrank.
ish bin ZAY-krahnk.

AIRPLANE

187. Is there bus service to the airport?
Gibt es einen Zubringerdienst zum Flughafen?
gipt es Ī-nen TSOO-bring-er-deenst tsoom FLOOK-hah-fen?

188. At what time will they pick me up?
Um wieviel Uhr wird man mich abholen?
oom VEE-feel oor veert mahn mish AHP-ho-len?

189. Is flight twenty-three on time?
Kommt Flug dreiundzwanzig pünktlich an?
kawmt flook DRĪ-oont-TSVAHN-tsish PEWNKT-lish AHN?

190. How many kilos may I take?
Wieviel Kilo darf ich mitnehmen?
VEE-feel KEE-lo dahrf ish MIT-nay-men?

191. How much per kilo for excess?
Wieviel kostet Übergewicht pro Kilo?
VEE-feel KAW-stet EW-ber-geh-visht pro KEE-lo?

TRAIN

SIDE TWO, BAND 3

192. Where is the railroad station?
Wo ist der Bahnhof?
vo ist dehr BAHN-hohf?

193. When does the boat-train for Bremerhaven leave?
Wann geht der Verbindungszug zum Schiff nach Bremerhaven?
vahn gayt der fehr-BIN-doongs-tsook tsoom shif nahkh bray-mer-HAH-fen?

194. From what track does the train leave?
Von welchem Bahnsteig fährt der Zug ab?
fun VEL-shem BAHN-shtik fehrt dehr tsook AHP?

195. Please open the window.
Bitte, öffnen Sie das Fenster.
BIT-tuh, ERF-nen zee dahs FEN-ster.

196. Close the window.
Schliessen Sie das Fenster!
SHLEES-sen zee dahs FEN-ster!

197. Where is [the diner]?
Wo ist [der Speisewagen]?
vo ist [dehr SHPĪ-zuh-vah-gen]?

198. —— the first-class sleeper.
der Schlafwagen.
dehr SHLAHF-vah-gen.

199. —— the second-class sleeper.
der Liegewagen.
dehr LEE-guh-vah-gen.

200. —— the smoking car.
das Raucherabteil.
dahs ROW-kher-ahp-tīl.

201. May I smoke?
Darf ich rauchen?
dahrf ish ROW-khen?

BUS AND STREETCAR

202. What streetcar goes to the Augusta Anlage?
Welche Strassenbahn fährt nach der Augusta Anlage?
VEL-shuh SHTRAH-sen-bahn fehrt nahkh dehr ow-GŎOS-tah AHN-lah-guh?

203. The bus stop.
Die Omnibus-Haltestelle.
dee AWM-nih-boos-hahl-tuh-shtel-luh.

204. A transfer.
Eine Umsteigekarte.
Ī-nuh OOM-shtī-guh-KAHR-tuh.

205. Where do I get the subway for Chestnut Avenue?
Wo finde ich die Untergrundbahn zur Kastanienallee?
vo FIN-duh ish dee OON-ter-groont-bahn tsoor kah-STAHN-yen-ahl-LAY?

206. Do you go near Bismarck Square?
Fahren Sie in die Nähe des Bismarckplatzes?
FAH-ren zee in dee NAY-uh des BIS-mahrk-PLAHT-tses?

207. Do I have to change?
Muss ich umsteigen?
moos ish OOM-shtī-gen?

208. Driver, please tell me where to get off.
Fahrer, bitte sagen Sie mir, wo ich aussteigen muss.
FAH-rer, BIT-tuh ZAH-gen zee meer, vo ish OWS-shtī-gen moos.

209. The next stop, please.
Die nächste Haltestelle, bitte.
dee NAYK-stuh HAHL-tuh-shtel-luh, BIT-tuh.

TAXI

210. Please call a taxi for me.
Bitte, rufen Sie mir ein Taxi.
BIT-tuh, ROO-fen zee meer īn TAHK-see.

211. Are you free?
Sind Sie frei?
zint zee frī?

212. What do you charge [per hour] per kilometer?
Was berechnen Sie [pro Stunde] pro Kilometer?
vahs beh-RES̅H̅-nen zee [pro SHTOON-duh] pro kil-o-MAY-ter?

213. Please drive [more slowly] more carefully.
Bitte fahren Sie [langsamer] vorsichtiger.
BIT-tuh FAH-ren zee [LAHNG-zah-mer] FOR-zis̅h̅-tih-ger.

214. Stop here.
Halten Sie hier!
HAHL-ten zee HEER!

215. Wait for me.
Warten Sie auf mich!
VAHR-ten zee owf mis̅h̅!

AUTOMOBILE TRAVEL *

SIDE TWO, BAND 4

216. Where can I rent a car?
Wo kann ich ein Auto mieten?
vo kahn is̅h̅ īn OW-toh MEE-ten?

217. I have an international driver's license.
Ich habe einen internationalen Führerschein.
is̅h̅ HAH-buh Ī-nen in-tehr-nahts-yo-NAH-len FEW-rehr-shīn.

* A complete list of road signs appears on pages 118–20.

218. A gas station.
Eine Tankstelle.
Ī-nuh TAHNK-shtel-luh.

219. A garage.
Eine Garage.
Ī-nuh gah-RAH-zhuh.

220. A mechanic.
Ein Mechaniker.
īn meh-SHAH-nih-ker.

221. Is the road [good] bad?
Ist die Strasse [gut] schlecht?
ist dee SHTRAH-suh [goot] shlesht?

222. Where does that road go?
Wohin führt die Strasse dort?
vo-HIN fewrt dee SHTRAH-suh dort?

223. What town is this?
Wie heisst diese Stadt?
vee hīst DEE-zuh shtaht?

224. The next city.
Die nächste Stadt.
dee NAYK-stuh shtaht.

225. Can you show me on the map?
Können Sie es mir auf der Karte zeigen?
KER-nen zee es meer owf dehr KAHR-tuh TSĪ-gen?

226. How much is gas a liter?
Wieviel kostet ein Liter Benzin?
VEE-feel KAW-stet īn LEE-ter ben-TSEEN?

227. The tank is [empty] full.
Der Tank ist [leer] voll.
dehr tahnk ist [layr] fawl.

228. Give me forty liters.
Geben Sie mir vierzig Liter!
GAY-ben zee meer FEER-tsish LEE-ter!

229. Please [check] change the oil.
Bitte [kontrollieren] wechseln Sie das Öl!
BIT-tuh [kawn-trawl-LEE-ren] VEK-seln zee dahs erl!

230. Please put water in the battery.
Füllen Sie bitte die Batterie mit Wasser auf!
FEWL-len zee BIT-tuh dee baht-teh-REE mit VAHS-ser OWF!

231. Will you lubricate the car, please?
Schmieren Sie bitte das Auto!
SHMEE-ren zee BIT-tuh dahs OW-toh!

232. Please wash the windshield.
Waschen Sie bitte die Windscheibe!
VAH-shen zee BIT-tuh dee VINT-shi-buh!

233. Adjust the brakes.
Stellen Sie die Bremsen nach!
SHTEL-len zee dee BREM-sen nahkh!

234. Will you please check the air?
Bitte, prüfen Sie die Luft!
BIT-tuh, PREW-fen zee dee looft!

235. Can you fix the flat tire?
Können Sie den beschädigten Reifen reparieren?
KERN-nen zee dayn beh-SHAY-dish-ten RI-fen reh-pah-REE-ren?

236. The engine overheats.
Der Motor wird zu heiss.
dehr mo-TOR veert tsoo his.

237. The motor [misses] stalls.
Der Motor [stottert] bleibt stehen.
dehr mo-TOR [STAW-tehrt] blīpt SHTAY-en.

238. May I park here for a while?
Kann ich hier eine Zeitlang parken?
kahn ish heer Ī-nuh TSĪT-lahng PAHR-ken?

PARTS OF THE CAR

SIDE THREE, BAND I

239. The accelerator. Der Gashebel.
dehr GAHS-hay-bel.

240. The battery. Die Batterie. *dee baht-teh-REE.*

241. The clutch. Das Kupplungspedal.
dahs KOOP-loongs-peh-dahl.

242. The gear shift. Der Schalthebel.
dehr SHAHLT-hay-bel.

243. The headlight. Der Scheinwerfer.
dehr SHĪN-vehr-fer.

244. The horn. Die Hupe. *dee HOO-puh.*

245. The spare tire. Der Reservereifen.
dehr reh-ZEHR-veh-RĪ-fen.

246. The spring. Die Feder. *dee FAY-der.*

247. The starter. Der Anlasser. *dehr AHN-lahs-ser.*

248. The steering wheel. Das Steuerrad.
dahs SHTOY-er-raht.

249. The wheel. Das Rad. *dahs raht.*

250. The (emergency) brake. Die (Hand-)Bremse.
dee (HAHNT-)BREM-suh.

HOTEL

SIDE THREE, BAND 2

251. I am looking for [a good hotel].
Ich suche [ein gutes Hotel].
ish ZOO-khuh [in GOO-tes ho-TEL].

252. —— the best hotel.
das beste Hotel.
dahs BES-tuh ho-TEL.

253. —— an inexpensive hotel.
ein billiges Hotel.
in BIL-lig-es ho-TEL.

254. —— a boarding house.
eine Pension.
I-nuh pen-SYOHN.

255. —— a furnished apartment.
eine möblierte Wohnung.
I-nuh mer-BLEER-tuh VO-noong.

256. I (do not) want to be in the center of town.
Ich möchte (nicht) im Zentrum der Stadt sein.
ish MERSH-tuh (nisht) im TSEN-troom dehr shtaht zin.

257. Where it is quiet.
Wo es ruhig ist.
vo es ROO-ish ist.

258. I have a reservation for today.
Ich habe eine Vorbestellung für heute.
ish HAH-buh I-nuh FOR-beh-shtel-loong fewr HOY-tuh.

259. Is there a vacancy?
Ist noch etwas frei?
ist nawkh ET-vahs frī?

260. Do you have a [room]?
Haben Sie [ein Zimmer]?
HAH-ben zee [īn TSIM-mer]?

261. —— a single room.
ein Einzelzimmer.
īn ĪN-tsel-tsim-mer.

262. —— a double room.
ein Doppelzimmer.
īn DAWP-pel-tsim-mer.

263. —— an air-conditioned room.
ein Zimmer mit Kühlanlage.
īn TSIM-mer mit KEWL-ahn-lah-guh.

264. I want a room [with a double bed].
Ich möchte ein Zimmer [mit einem Doppelbett].
ish MERSH-tuh īn TSIM-mer [mit Ī-nem DAWP-pel-bet].

265. —— with twin beds.
mit zwei Einzelbetten.
mit tsvī ĪN-tsel-bet-ten.

266. —— with a bath.
mit Bad.
mit baht.

267. —— with running water.
mit fliessendem Wasser.
mit FLEE-sen-dem VAHS-ser.

268. I want a room [without meals].
Ich möchte ein Zimmer [ohne Mahlzeiten].
ish MERSH-tuh in TSIM-mer [OH-nuh MAHL-tsi-ten].

269. —— for tonight.
für heute Nacht.
fewr HOY-tuh nahkht.

270. —— for several days.
für mehrere Tage.
fewr MAY-reh-ruh TAH-guh.

271. —— for two persons.
für zwei Personen.
fewr tsvi pehr-ZO-nen.

272. I should like to see the room.
Ich möchte das Zimmer gern sehen.
ish MERSH-tuh dahs TSIM-mer gehrn ZAY-en.

273. Is it [upstairs] downstairs?
Ist es [oben] unten?
ist es [O-ben] OON-ten?

274. Is there an elevator?
Gibt es einen Fahrstuhl?
gipt es I-nen FAHR-shtool?

275. Room service, please.
Zimmerbedienung, bitte.
TSIM-mer-beh-DEE-noong, BIT-tuh.

276. Please send [a porter] to my room.
Bitte schicken Sie [den Hausdiener] auf mein Zimmer.
BIT-tuh SHIK-ken zee [dayn HOWS-dee-ner] owf min TSIM-mer.

277. —— **a chambermaid.**
ein Zimmermädchen.
īn TSIM-mer-mayd-shen.

278. —— **a bellhop.**
ein Hotelpage.
īn ho-TEL-pah-zhuh.

279. Please wake me at nine fifteen.
Bitte wecken Sie mich um neun Uhr fünfzehn.
BIT-tuh VEK-ken zee mish oom noyn oor FEWNF-tsayn.

280. I should like to have breakfast in my room.
Ich möchte auf meinem Zimmer frühstücken.
ish MERSH-tuh owf MĪ-nem TSIM-mer FREW-shtewk-ken.

281. Who is it?
Wer ist es?
vehr ist es?

282. Come back a little later.
Kommen Sie ein wenig später.
KAWM-men zee īn VAY-nish SHPAY-ter.

283. Brink me [a blanket].
Bringen Sie mir [eine Decke].
BRING-en zee meer [Ī-nuh DEK-kuh].

284. —— **a pillow.**
ein Kissen.
īn KIS-sen.

285. —— **a pillowcase.**
einen Kissenbezug.
Ī-nen KIS-sen-beh-tsook.

286. —— **sheets.**
Laken.
LAH-ken.

287. —— **hangers.**
Kleiderbügel.
KLĪ-der-BEW-gel.

288. —— **soap.**
Seife.
ZĪ-fuh.

289. —— **towels.**
Handtücher.
HAHNT-tew-s̄h̄er.

290. —— **a bath mat.**
einen Badeteppich.
Ī-nen BAH-duh-tep-pis̄h̄.

291. —— **toilet paper.**
Toilettenpapier.
Toh-ah-LET-ten-pah-peer.

292. I would like to speak to the manager.
Ich möchte mit dem Hoteldirektor sprechen.
is̄h̄ MĒRS̄H̄-tuh mit daym ho-TEL-dee-rek-tor SHPREH-s̄h̄en.

293. My room key.
Mein Zimmerschlüssel.
mīn TSIM-mer-shlews-sel.

294. Have I any letters or messages?
Sind Briefe oder Bestellungen für mich da?
zint BREE-fuh O-der beh-SHTEL-loong-en fewr mis̄h̄ dah?

295. What is my room number?
Was ist meine Zimmernummer?
vahs ist MĪ-nuh TSIM-mer-noom-mer?

296. I am leaving at two o'clock in the afternoon. (*fourteen o'clock*).
Ich fahre um vierzehn Uhr ab.
ish FAH-ruh oom FEER-tsayn oor AHP.

297. Please make out my bill as soon as possible.
Bitte machen Sie meine Rechnung fertig, so bald wie möglich.
BIT-tuh MAH-khen zee MĪ-nuh RESH-noong FEHR-tish, zo bahlt vee MERG-lish.

298. Are room service and tax included?
Sind Bedienung und Steuer einbegriffen?
zint beh-DEE-noong oont SHTOY-er ĪN-beh-grif-fen?

299. Please forward my mail to this address:
Bitte schicken Sie meine Post an diese Adresse nach:
BIT-tuh SHIK-ken zee MĪ-nuh pawst ahn DEE-zuh ah-DRES-suh nahkh:

AT THE CAFÉ

SIDE THREE, BAND 3

300. Bartender, I would like [a drink].
Barkellner, ich möchte [ein Getränk].
BAHR-kel-ner, ish MERSH-tuh [īn geh-TRENK].

301. —— a cocktail.
einen Cocktail.
Ī-nen "cocktail."

302. —— **a bottle of mineral water.**
eine Flasche Mineralwasser.
Ī-nuh FLAH-shuh mee-neh-RAHL-vahs-ser.

303. —— **a glass of sherry.**
ein Glas Sherry.
īn glahs "sherry."

304. —— [**light**] **dark beer.**
[helles] dunkles Bier.
[HEL-les] DOONK-les beer.

305. —— **whiskey and soda.**
Whisky mit Selter.
VIS-kee mit ZEL-ter.

306. —— **brandy.**
Schnapps.
shnahps.

307. —— **white wine.**
Weisswein.
VĪS-vīn.

308. —— **red wine.**
Rotwein.
ROHT-vīn.

309. —— **champagne.**
Champagner.
shahm-PAHN-yer.

310. —— **a liqueur.**
ein Likör.
īn lee-KERR.

311. Let's have another round.
Noch eine Runde.
nawhk Ī-nuh ROON-duh.

312. Cheers!
Prosit!
PRO-zit!

313. To your health!
Zum Wohl!
tsoom vohl!

AT THE RESTAURANT

SIDE THREE, BAND 4

314. Can you recommend a good restaurant [for dinner]?
Können Sie ein gutes Restaurant [fürs Abendessen] empfehlen?
KERN-nen zee in GOO-tes res-toh-RAHNG [fewrs AH-bent-es-sen] emp-FAY-len?

315. —— for breakfast.
fürs Frühstück.
fewrs FREW-shtewk.

316. —— for lunch.
fürs Mittagessen.
fewrs MIT-tahk-es-sen.

317. I want only a sandwich.
Ich möchte nur ein belegtes Brot essen.
ish MERSH-tuh noor in beh-LAYK-tes broht ES-sen.

318. At what time is supper served?
Wann wird das Abendbrot serviert?
vahn veert dahs AH-bent-broht sehr-VEERT?

319. Are you [my waiter]?
Sind Sie [mein Kellner]?
zint zee [min KEL-ner]?

320. —— my waitress.
meine Kellnerin.
mī-nuh KEL-ner-in.

321. —— the headwaiter.
der Oberkellner.
dehr O-ber-kel-ner.

322. Waiter!
Herr Ober!
hehr O-ber!

323. Waitress!
Fräulein!
FROY-līn!

324. Give me a table near the window, please.
Geben Sie mir bitte einen Tisch in der Nähe des Fensters.
GAY-ben zee meer BIT-tuh Ī-nen tish in dehr NAY-uh des FEN-sters.

325. We want to dine à la carte.
Wir wollen à la carte speisen.
veer VAWL-len "à la carte" SHPĪ-zen.

326. We want to dine table d'hôte.
Wir wollen das Menü essen.
veer VAWL-len dahs meh-NEW ES-sen.

327. Please serve us quickly.
Bitte, bedienen Sie uns schnell.
BIT-tuh, beh-DEE-nen zee oons shnel.

328. Bring me [the menu].
Bringen Sie mir [die Speisekarte].
BRING-en zee meer [dee SHPĪ-zuh-kahr-tuh].

329. —— **the wine list.**
die Weinkarte.
dee VĪN-kahr-tuh.

330. —— **a napkin.**
eine Serviette.
Ī-nuh zehrv-YET-tuh.

331. —— **a fork.**
eine Gabel.
Ī-nuh GAH-bel.

332. —— **a knife.**
ein Messer.
īn MES-ser.

333. —— **a plate.**
einen Teller.
Ī-nen TEL-ler.

334. —— **a teaspoon.**
einen Teelöffel.
Ī-nen TAY-le̅r-fel.

335. —— **a soup spoon.**
einen Suppenlöffel.
Ī-nen ZOOP-pen-le̅rf-fel.

336. **I would like something [plain].**
Ich möchte etwas [Einfaches] essen.
is̅h ME̅RS̅H-tuh ET-vahs [ĪN-fah-khes] ES-sen.

337. —— **not too spicy.**
nicht zu Scharfes.
nis̅ht tsoo SHAHRF-es.

338. —— **not too sweet.**
nicht zu Süsses.
nis̅ht tsoo ZEWS-ses.

339. —— without fat.
Fettfreies.
FET-frī-es.

340. —— cooked (or boiled).
Gekochtes.
geh-KAWKH-tes.

341. —— fried.
Gebratenes.
geh-BRAH-teh-nes.

342. I like the meat [rare].
Ich möchte das Fleisch [rosa].
ish̄ MĒRSH̄-tuh dahs flīsh RO-zah.

343. ——medium.
halb durchgebraten.
hahlp DOORSH̄-geh-brah-ten.

344. —— well done.
gut durchgebraten.
goot DOORSH̄-geh-brah-ten.

345. Enjoy your meal!
Guten Appetit!
GOO-ten ahp-peh-TEET!

346. A little more.
Ein bisschen mehr.
īn BIS-sh̄en mehr.

347. Enough.
Genug.
geh-NOOK.

348. Too much.
Zu viel.
tsoo feel.

349. This is not clean.
Das is nicht sauber.
dahs ist nisht ZOW-ber.

350. This is cold.
Das ist kalt.
dahs ist kahlt.

351. I did not order this.
Ich habe dies nicht bestellt.
ish HAH-buh dees nisht beh-SHTELT.

352. Take it away, please.
Nehmen Sie es fort, bitte.
NAY-men zee es fort, BIT-tuh.

353. May I change this for a salad?
Können Sie stattdessen einen Salat bringen?
KER-nen zee staht-DES-sen Ī-nen zah-LAHT BRING-en?

354. The check, please.
Die Rechnung, bitte.
dee RESH-noong, BIT-tuh.

355. Is the tip included?
Ist die Bedienung einbegriffen?
ist dee beh-DEE-noong ĪN-beh-grif-fen?

356. There is a mistake in the bill.
Es ist ein Fehler in der Rechnung.
es ist īn FAY-ler in dehr RESH-noong.

357. What are these charges for?
Wofür ist dies berechnet?
VO-fewr ist dees beh-RESH-net?

358. Keep the change.
Behalten Sie den Rest.
beh-HAHL-ten zee dayn rest.

359. The food and service were excellent.
Das Essen und die Bedienung waren ausgezeichnet.
dahs ES-sen oont dee beh-DEE-noong VAH-ren OWS-geh-tsish-net.

FOOD LIST

360. Please bring me some water.
Bitte, bringen Sie mir Wasser.
BIT-tuh BRING-en zee meer VAHS-ser.

361. With ice.
Mit Eis.
mit is.

362. Bread.
Brot.
broht.

363. Butter.
Butter.
BOOT-ter.

364. Sugar.
Zucker.
TSOOK-ker.

365. Salt.
Salz.
zahlts.

366. Pepper.
Pfeffer.
PFEF-fer.

367. Oil.
Öl.
erl.

368. Vinegar.
Essig.
ES-sish.

369. Mustard.
Senf.
zenf.

370. Gravy.
Sosse.
ZOH-suh.

BREAKFAST FOODS

371. May I have some [fruit juice]?
Kann ich etwas [Fruchtsaft] haben?
kahn ish ET-vahs [FROOKHT-zahft] HAH-ben?

372. —— orange juice.
Apfelsinensaft.
ahp-fel-ZEE-nen-zahft.

373. —— tomato juice.
Tomatensaft.
taw-MAH-ten-zahft.

374. —— stewed prunes.
gekochte Dörrzwetschen.
geh-KAWKH-tuh DERR-tsvet-shen.

375. —— oatmeal.
Haferschleim.
HAH-fer-shlim.

376. —— toast and jam.
Toast und Marmelade.
tohst oont mahr-meh-LAH-duh.

377. —— **rolls.**
Brötchen.
BRERT-shen.

378. —— **an omelet.**
ein Omelett.
in awm-LET.

379. —— **soft-boiled eggs.**
weich gekochte Eier.
vish geh-KAWKH-tuh I-er.

380. —— **four-minute eggs.**
gekochte Eier. Vier Minuten.
geh-KAWKH-tuh I-er. feer mih-NOO-ten.

381. —— **hard-boiled eggs.**
harte Eier.
HAHR-tuh I-er.

382. —— **scrambled eggs.**
Rühreier.
REWR-i-er.

383. —— **fried eggs.**
Spiegeleier.
SHPEE-gel-i-er.

384. —— **ham and eggs.**
Eier mit Schinken.
I-er mit SHINK-en.

SOUPS AND ENTRÉES

SIDE FOUR, BAND 1

385. I want some [chicken soup].
Ich möchte [Hühnersuppe].
ish MERSH-tuh [HEW-ner-zoop-puh].

386. —— **vegetable soup.**
Gemüsesuppe.
geh-MEW-zuh-zoop-puh.

387. —— **beef.**
Rindfleisch.
RINT-flīsh.

388. —— **roast beef.**
Roastbeef.
"*roast beef.*"

389. —— **roast chicken.**
Brathuhn.
BRAHT-hoon.

390. —— **duck.**
Ente.
EN-tuh.

391. —— **fish.**
Fisch.
fish.

392. —— **goose.**
Gans.
gahns.

393. —— **lamb.**
Lamm.
lahm.

394. —— **liver.**
Leber.
LAY-ber.

395. —— **lobster.**
Hummer.
HOOM-mer.

396. —— **oysters.**
Austern.
OW-stern.

397. —— **pork.**
Schwein.
shvīn.

398. —— **sardines.**
Sardinen.
zahr-DEE-nen.

399. —— **sausage.**
Wurst.
voorst.

400. —— **shrimps.**
Krabben.
KRAHB-ben.

401. —— **Steak.**
Steak.
"*steak.*"

402. —— **veal.**
Kalb.
kahlp.

VEGETABLES AND SALAD

403. I want some [asparagus].
Ich möchte [Spargel].
ish MERSH-tuh [SHPAHR-gel].

404. —— **beans.**
Bohnen.
BOH-nen.

405. —— **cabbage.**
Kohl.
kohl.

406. —— **carrots.**
Karotten.
kah-RAWT-ten.

407. —— **cauliflower.**
Blumenkohl.
BLOO-men-kohl

408. —— **cucumbers.**
Gurken.
GOOR-ken.

409. —— **lettuce.**
Kopfsalat.
KAWPF-zah-laht.

410. —— **mushrooms.**
Pilze.
PIL-tsuh.

411. —— **onions.**
Zwiebeln.
TSVEE-beln.

412. —— **peas.**
Erbsen.
EHRP-sen.

413. —— **peppers.**
Pfefferschoten.
PFEF-fer-SHOH-ten.

414. —— **boiled potatoes.**
Salzkartoffeln.
ZAHLTS-kahr-tawf-feln.

415. —— **mashed potatoes.**
Kartoffelpüree.
kahr-TAWF-fel-pew-ray.

416. —— **fried potatoes.**
Bratkartoffeln.
BRAHT-kahr-tawf-feln.

417. —— **rice.**
Reis.
rīs.

418. —— **spinach.**
Spinat.
shpin-AHT.

419. —— **tomatoes.**
Tomaten.
toh-MAH-ten.

FRUITS

420. **Do you have [cherries]?**
Haben Sie [Kirschen]?
HAH-ben zee [KEER-shen]?

421. —— **an apple.**
einen Apfel.
Ī-nen AHP-fel.

422. —— **a grapefruit.**
eine Pampelmuse.
Ī-nuh pahm-pel-MOO-zuh.

423. —— **grapes.**
Trauben.
TROW-ben.

424. —— melon.
eine Melone.
Ī-nuh meh-LO-nuh.

425. —— an orange.
eine Apfelsine.
Ī-nuh ahp-fel-ZEE-nuh.

426. —— a peach.
einen Pfirsich.
Ī-nen PFEER-zish.

427. —— raspberries.
Himbeeren.
HIM-bay-ren.

428. —— strawberries.
Erdbeeren.
EHRT-bay-ren.

BEVERAGES

429. A cup of black coffee.
Eine Tasse schwarzen Kaffee.
Ī-nuh TAHS-suh SHVAHR-tsen kahf-FAY.

430. Coffee with cream.
Kaffee mit Sahne.
kah-FAY mit ZAH-nuh.

431. A glass of milk.
Ein Glas Milch.
īn glahs milsh.

432. Tea with lemon.
Tee mit Zitrone.
tay mit tsih-TRO-nuh.

433. Lemonade.
Limonade.
lee-maw-NAH-duh.

434. Soft drinks.
Alkoholfreie Getränke.
AHL-ko-hohl-frī-uh geh-TRENG-kuh.

DESSERTS

435. I should like [some cake].
Ich möchte [ein Stück Kuchen].
ish MERSH-tuh [īn shtewk KOO-khen].

436. —— a piece of pie.
ein Stück Torte.
īn shtewk TOR-tuh.

437. —— cheese.
Käse.
KAY-zuh.

438. —— cookies.
Kekse.
KEK-suh.

439. —— chocolate ice cream.
Schokoladeneis.
shaw-kaw-LAH-den-īs.

440. —— vanilla ice cream.
Vanilleeis.
vah-NIL-luh-īs.

CONVERSATION AT THE RESTAURANT

(At normal rate of speech)

SIDE FOUR, BAND 2

441. **Möchten Sie etwas trinken?**
Would you like something to drink?

442. **Ja, bitte bringen Sie uns einen Wermut und ein Bier.**
Yes, please bring us a vermouth and a beer.

443. **Dürfte ich jetzt Ihre weitere Bestellungen entgegennehmen?**
May I take the rest of your order now?

444. **Was würden Sie empfehlen? Was ist Ihre Spezialität?**
What would you recommend? What is the specialty of the house?

445. **Der Kalbsbraten ist heute besonders gut. Die Forelle ist auch sehr zu empfehlen.**
The veal roast is especially good today. I can also highly recommend the trout.

446. **Gut, bringen Sie uns eine Portion Kalbsbraten und einmal Rehrücken.**
All right, bring us one order of veal roast and one of saddle of venison.

447. **Jawohl, mein Herr, und welche Beilagen wünschen die Herrschaften?**
Yes, sir, and what sidedishes would the lady and gentleman like with that?

448. **Mit dem Kalbsbraten bringen Sie mir bitte Bratkartoffeln und Rosenkohl und mit dem Rehrücken, Rotkohl. Und mit dem**

Hauptgang möchten wir eine Flasche Moselwein.

Bring me home-fried potatoes and Brussels sprouts with the veal roast, and with the saddle of venison, red cabbage. And we would like a bottle of Moselle wine with our main course.

449. **Welche Vorspeise und Suppe wünschen Sie?**

Which appetizer and soup do you wish?

450. **Russische Eier und Gänseleberpastete. Dann Erbsensuppe und einmal Fruchtsuppe.**

Eggs à la Russe and pâté de foie gras. Then pea soup and one portion of fruit soup.

451. **Möchten Sie auch Salat?**

Would you also like some salad?

452. **Ja, eine Portion gemischten Salat und einmal grünen Salat mit ein wenig Essig und Öl.**

Yes, one mixed salad and one order of lettuce with a little oil and vinegar.

453. **Als Nachspeise haben wir Eis, diverses Gebäck, Pflaumenkuchen und Obst.**

For dessert we have: ice cream, assorted pastry, plum cake, and fruit.

454. **Schön. Einmal Schokoladeneis und ein Stück Pflaumenkuchen. Eine Tasse Kaffee und eine Tasse Tee mit Sahne. Und Fräulein, bringen Sie uns noch einen Teelöffel. Dieser hier ist nicht ganz sauber.**

Very well. One chocolate ice cream and one piece of plum cake. One cup of coffee and one cup of tea with cream. And waitress, bring another spoon. This one is not quite clean.

456. Bitte entschuldigen Sie.
Please excuse me.

457. Können Sie mir bitte die Rechnung bringen? Wir möchten ins Theater und es ist höchste Zeit.
Can you please bring the bill? We want to go to the theatre and it is getting late.

458. Jawohl, mein Herr.
Yes, sir.

CHURCH

SIDE FOUR, BAND 3

459. Is there an English-speaking [priest, rabbi] minister?
Gibt es einen englisch-sprechenden [Priester, Rabbiner] Geistlichen?
gipt es Ī-nen ENG-lish SHPRESH-en-den [PREE-ster, rah-BEE-ner] GĪST-lih-shen?

460. A [Catholic] Protestant Church.
Eine [katholische] protestantische Kirche.
Ī-nuh [kah-TOH-lih-shuh] pro-tes-TAHN-tih-shuh KEER-shuh.

461. An Anglican church.
Eine anglikanische Kirche.
Ī-nuh ahng-lih-KAH-nih-shuh KEER-shuh.

462. A synagogue.
Eine Synagoge.
Ī-nuh zew-nah-GO-guh.

463. When is [the service] the mass?
Wann ist [der Gottesdienst] die Messe?
vahn ist [dehr GAWT-tes-deenst] dee MES-suh?

SIGHTSEEING

464. I want a licensed guide who speaks English.
Ich möchte einen offiziellen, englisch-sprechenden Reiseführer.
ish MERSH-tuh Ī-nen awf-fits-YEL-len, ENG-lish-shpreh-shen-den RĪ-zuh-few-rer.

465. What is the charge [per hour] per day?
Was sind die Gebühren [pro Stunde] pro Tag?
vahs zint dee geh-BEW-ren [pro SHTOON-duh] pro tahk?

466. I am interested [in architecture].
Ich interessiere mich [für Architektur].
ish in-teh-reh-SEE-ruh mish [fewr ahr-shih-tek-TOOR].

467. —— in painting.
für Malerei.
fewr mah-leh-RĪ.

468. —— in sculpture.
für Bildhauerei.
fewr BILT-how-er-RĪ.

469. Show us [the castle].
Zeigen Sie uns [das Schloss].
TSĪ-gen zee oons [dahs shlaws].

470. —— **the cathedral.**
den Dom.
dayn dohm.

471. —— **the museums.**
die Museen.
dee moo-ZAY-en.

472. When does it [open] close?
Wann wird [geöffnet] geschlossen?
vahn veert [geh-ERF-net] geh-SHLAWS-sen?

473. Where is the [entrance] exit?
Wo ist der [Eingang] Ausgang?
vo ist dehr [IN-gahng] OWS-gahng?

AMUSEMENTS

SIDE 4, BAND 4

474. I should like to go [to a concert].
Ich möchte [in ein Konzert] gehen.
ish MERSH-tuh [in in kawn-TSEHRT] GAY-en.

475. —— **to a matinee.**
zu einer Matinee.
tsoo I-ner mah-tee-NAY.

476. —— **to the movies.**
ins Kino.
ins KEE-no.

477. —— **to a night club.**
in ein Nachtlokal.
in in NAHKHT-lo-kahl.

478. —— **to the opera.**
in die Oper.
in dee O-per.

479. —— to the theatre.
ins Theater.
ins tay-AH-ter.

480. —— to the box office.
zur Theaterkasse.
tsoor tay-AH-ter-kahs-suh.

481. What is playing tonight?
Was wird heute abend gegeben?
vahs veert HOY-tuh AH-bent geh-GAY-ben?

482. Is there an evening performance on holidays?
Findet eine Abendvorstellung an Feiertagen statt?
FIN-det Ī-nuh AH-bent-for-shtel-loong ahn FĪ-er-tah-gen shtaht?

483. When does the floorshow start?
Wann fängt die Revue an?
vahn fenkt dee REH-vew AHN?

484. Have you [any seats] for tonight?
Haben Sie [noch Plätze] für heute Abend?
HAH-ben zee [nawkh PLET-suh] fewr HOY-tuh AH-bent?

485. —— an orchestra seat.
einen Parkettplatz.
Ī-nen pahr-KET-plahts.

486. —— a box.
eine Loge.
Ī-nuh LO-zhuh.

487. In the balcony.
Im Balkon.
im bahl-KOHN.

488. Can I see well from there?
Kann ich dort gut sehen?
kahn ish dort goot ZAY-en?

489. Where can we go to dance?
Wo können wir tanzen?
vo KERN-nen veer TAHN-tsen?

490. What is [the cover charge]?
Wieviel ist [der Gedeckzuschlag]?
VEE-feel ist [dehr geh-DEK-tsoo-shlahk]?

491. —— the minimum charge.
der Mindestpreis.
dehr MIN-dest-pris.

492. May I have this dance?
Darf ich um diesen Tanz bitten?
dahrf ish oom DEE-zen tahnts BIT-ten?

SPORTS

493. Let's go [to the beach].
Lasst uns [zum Strand] gehen.
lahst oons [tsoom shtrahnt] GAY-en.

494. —— to the horse races.
zum Pferderennen.
tsoom PFEHR-duh-ren-nen.

495. —— to the swimming pool.
zum Schwimmbad.
tsoom SHVIM-baht.

496. I'd like to play [golf] tennis.
Ich möchte [Golf] Tennis spielen.
ish MERSH-tuh ["golf"] TEN-nis SHPEE-len.

497. Can we go [fishing]?
Können wir [angeln]?
KERN-nen veer [AHNG-eln]?

498. —— horseback riding.
reiten.
RĪ-ten.

499. —— skating.
schlittschuhlaufen.
SHLIT-shoo-low-fen.

500. —— skiing.
skilaufen.
SHEE-low-fen.

501. —— swimming.
schwimmen.
SHVIM-men.

BANK AND MONEY

SIDE 4, BAND 5

502. Where is the nearest bank?
Wo ist die nächste Bank?
vo ist dee NAYK-stuh bahnk?

503. At which window can I cash this?
An welchem Schalter kann ich dies einlösen?
ahn VEL-shem SHAHL-ter kahn ish dees ĪN-ler-zen?

504. Will you cash [this personal check]?
Würden Sie bitte [diesen Scheck auf mein Privatkonto] einlösen?
VEWR-den zee BIT-tuh [DEE-zen shek owf mīn pree-VAHT-kawn-toh] ĪN-ler-zen?

505. —— a traveler's check?
einen Reisescheck.
Ī-nen RĪ-zuh-shek.

506. What is the exchange rate on the dollar?
Wie steht der Dollar im Kurs?
vee shtayt dehr DAWL-lahr im koors?

507. Can you change this for me?
Können Sie mir das wechseln?
KERN-nen zee meer dahs VEK-seln?

508. May I have fifty dollars' worth of German money?
Ich möchte fünfzig Dollar in deutsches Geld umwechseln.
ish MERSH-tuh FEWNF-tsish DAWL-lahr in DOYT-shes gelt OOM-vek-seln.

509. (Do not) give me many large bills.
Geben Sie mir (nicht) viele grosse Noten.
GAY-ben zee meer (nisht) FEE-luh GRO-suh NO-ten.

510. Can I have some small change?
Kann ich etwas Kleingeld haben?
kahn ish ET-vahs KLĪN-gelt HAH-ben?

SHOPPING

511. I want to go shopping.
Ich möchte einkaufen gehen.
ish MERSH-tuh ĪN-kow-fen GAY-en.

512. I (do not) like this one.
Dies gefällt mir (nicht).
dees geh-FELT meer (nisht).

513. How much is it?
Wieviel kostet es?
VEE-feel KAW-stet es?

514. I prefer something [better].
Ich möchte lieber etwas [Besseres] haben.
ish MERSH-tuh LEE-ber ET-vahs [BES-ser-
HAH-ben.

515. —— cheaper.
Billigeres.
BIL-lih-geh-res.

516. —— smaller.
Kleineres.
KLĪ-neh-res.

517. —— larger.
Grösseres.
GRER-seh-res.

518. Show me some others.
Zeigen Sie mir ein paar andere.
TSĪ-gen zee meer īn pahr AHN-deh-ruh.

519. At a more moderate price.
Die billiger sind.
dee BIL-lih-ger zint.

520. Is this your best price?
Ist dies Ihr letzter Preis?
ist dees eer LETS-ster prīs?

521. May I try this on?
Darf ich dies anprobieren?
dahrf ish dees AHN-pro-bee-ren?

522. Can I order size 32?
Kann ich Grösse zweiunddreissig bestellen?
kahn ish GRERS-suh TSVI-oont-DRI-sish beh-SHTEL-len?

523. Please take the measurements.
Bitte nehmen Sie Mass.
BIT-tuh NAY-men zee mahs.

524. Please measure [the length].
Bitte messen Sie [die Länge].
BIT-tuh MES-sen zee [dee LENG-uh].

525. —— the width.
die Breite.
dee BRI-tuh.

526. How long will it take?
Wie lange wird es dauern?
vee LAHNG-uh veert es DOW-ern?

527. I'll return later.
Ich werde später wiederkommen.
ish VEHR-duh SHPAY-ter VEE-der-kawm-men.

528. Can you ship it to New York City?
Können Sie es nach Neu York senden?
KER-nen zee es nahkh noy york ZEN-den?

529. Do I pay [the salesman]?
Soll ich [bei dem Verkäufer] bezahlen?
zawl ish [bi daym fer-KOY-fer] beh-TSAH-len?

530. —— the salesgirl.
bei der Verkäuferin.
bi dehr fer-KOY-feh-rin.

531. —— the cashier.
an der Kasse.
ahn dehr KAHS-suh.

532. Please send me a bill.
Bitte, schicken Sie mir eine Rechnung.
BIT-tuh, SHIK-ken zee meer Ī-nuh RESH-noong.

CLOTHING

SIDE FIVE, BAND I

533. I want to buy [a bathing cap].
Ich möchte [eine Bademütze] kaufen.
ish MERSH-tuh [Ī-nuh BAH-duh-mewt-tsuh] KOW-fen.

534. —— a bathing suit.
einen Badeanzug.
Ī-nen BAH-duh-ahn-tsook.

535. —— a blouse.
eine Bluse.
Ī-nuh BLOO-zuh.

536. —— a brassière.
einen Büstenhalter.
Ī-nen BEW-sten-hahl-ter.

537. —— an overcoat.
einen Wintermantel.
Ī-nen VIN-ter-mahn-tel.

538. —— a dress.
ein Kleid.
īn klīt.

539. —— some children's dresses.
Kinderkleider.
KIN-der-klī-der.

540. —— a pair of garters.
ein Paar Strumpfhalter.
īn pahr SHTROOMPF-hahl-ter.

541.—— **a pair of gloves.**
ein Paar Handschuhe.
īn pahr HAHNT-shoo-uh.

542. —— **a handbag.**
eine Damentasche.
Ī-nuh DAH-men-tah-shuh.

543. —— **one dozen handkerchiefs.**
ein Dutzend Taschentücher.
īn DŎŎ-tsend TAH-shen-tew-s̄her.

544. —— **a hat.**
einen Hut.
Ī-nen hoot.

545. —— **a jacket.**
eine Jacke.
Ī-nuh YAHK-kuh.

546. —— **some lingerie.**
etwas Damenwäsche.
ET-vahs DAH-men-veh-shuh.

547. —— **a nightgown.**
ein Nachthemd.
īn NAHKHT-hemt.

548. —— **a raincoat.**
einen Regenmantel.
Ī-nen RAY-gen-mahn-tel.

549. —— **a pair of shoes.**
ein Paar Schuhe.
īn pahr SHOO-uh.

550. —— **some shoelaces.**
Schnürsenkel.
SHNEWR-zen-kel.

551. —— **a skirt.**
einen Rock.
Ī-nen rawk.

552. —— **a pair of slippers.**
ein Paar Pantoffeln.
īn pahr pahn-TAWF-feln.

553. —— **a pair of socks.**
ein Paar Socken.
īn pahr ZAWK-en.

554. —— **a pair of nylon stockings.**
ein Paar Perlon Strümpfe.
īn pahr PEHR-lawn SHTREWMP-fuh.

555. —— **a shirt.**
ein Hemd.
īn hemt.

556. —— **a man's suit.**
einen Herrenanzug.
Ī-nen HEHR-ren-ahn-tsook.

557. —— **a sweater.**
einen Pullover.
Ī-nen POOL-o-ver.

558. —— **some neckties.**
einige Krawatten.
Ī-nih-guh krah-VAHT-ten.

559. —— **a pair of trousers.**
ein Paar Hosen.
īn pahr HO-zen.

560. —— **underwear.**
Unterwäsche.
OON-ter-veh-shuh.

SUNDRIES

561. Do you have [some ash trays]?
Haben Sie [Aschenbecher]?
zee [AH-shen-beh-sher]?

ts' supplies.
nenmaterialien.
TSĪ-shen-mah-teh-ree-AHL-yen.

563. —— a box of candy.
eine Schachtel Süssigkeiten.
Ī-nuh SHAHKH-tel ZEWS-sish-kī-ten.

564. —— some china.
etwas Geschirr.
ET-vahs geh-SHEER.

565. —— a silver compact.
eine silberne Puderdose.
Ī-nuh ZIL-ber-nuh POO-der-doh-zuh.

566. —— gold cuff links.
goldene Manschettenknöpfe.
GAWL-deh-nuh mahn-SHET-ten-knerp-fuh.

567. —— dolls.
Puppen.
POOP-pen.

568. —— earrings.
Ohrringe.
AWR-ring-uh.

569. —— sheet music.
Noten.
NO-ten.

570. —— **musical instruments.**
Musikinstrumente.
moo-ZEEK-in-shtroo-MEN-tuh.

571. —— **perfume.**
Parfüm.
pahr-FUN.

572. —— **pictures.**
Bilder.
BIL-der.

573. —— **a radio.**
ein Radio.
īn RAH-dee-o.

574. —— **records.**
Schallplatten.
SHAHL-plaht-ten.

575. —— **silverware.**
Silbersachen.
ZIL-ber-sah-khen.

576. —— **some souvenirs.**
ein paar Andenken.
īn pahr AHN-denk-en.

577. —— **a television set.**
einen Fernsehapparat.
Ī-nen FEHRN-zay-ah-pah-raht.

578. —— **toys.**
Spielsachen.
SHPEEL-zah-khen.

579. —— **a silk umbrella.**
einen seidenen Regenschirm.
Ī-nen ZĪ-deh-nen RAY-gen-sheerm.

580. —— a wristwatch.
eine Armbanduhr.
Ī-nuh AHRM-bahnt-oor.

COLORS

581. I want [a lighter shade].
Ich möchte [eine hellere Schattierung] haben.
ish MĒRSH-tuh [Ī-nuh HEL-leh-ruh shah-TEE-roong] HAH-ben.

582. —— a darker shade.
eine dunklere Schattierung.
Ī-nuh DOONK-leh-ruh shah-TEE-roong.

583. Black. Schwarz. *shvahrts.*

584. Blue. Blau. *blow.*

585. Brown. Braun. *brown.*

586. Gray. Grau. *grow.*

587. Green. Grün. *grewn.*

588. Orange. Orange. *aw-RAHN-zhuh.*

589. Pink. Rosa. *RO-zah.*

590. Purple. Lila. *LEE-lah.*

591. Red. Rot. *roht.*

592. White. Weiss. *vīs.*

593. Yellow. Gelb. *gelp.*

STORES *

594. Where is [the bakery].
Wo ist [die Bäckerei]?
vo ist [dee bek-eh-RĪ]?

* An extensive list of stores and services appears in the list *Signs and Public Notices* on pages 114–18.

595. —— **a candy store.**
ein Schokoladengeschäft.
ĭn shoh-koh-LAH-den-geh-sheft.

596. —— **a cigar store.**
ein Zigarrenladen.
ĭn tsih-GAHR-ren-lah-den.

597. —— **a clothing store.**
ein Kleidergeschäft.
ĭn KLĪ-der-geh-sheft.

598. —— **a department store.**
ein Kaufhaus.
ĭn KOWF-hows.

599. —— **a five-and-ten-cent store.**
ein Einheitspreisgeschäft.
ĭn ĪN-hīts-prīs-geh-sheft.

600. —— **a drugstore.**
eine Drogerie.
Ī-nuh dro-geh-REE.

601. —— **a pharmacy.**
eine Apotheke.
Ī-nuh ah-paw-TAY-kuh.

602. —— **a grocery.**
ein Lebensmittelgeschäft.
ĭn LAY-bens-mit-tel-geh-sheft.

603. —— **a hardware store.**
ein Eisenwarengeschäft.
ĭn Ī-zen-vah-ren-geh-sheft.

604. —— **a hat shop.**
ein Hutladen.
ĭn HOOT-lah-den.

605. —— **a jewelry store.**
ein Juweliergeschäft.
īn yoo-veh-LEER-geh-sheft.

606. —— **a market.**
ein Markt.
īn mahrkt.

607. —— **a meat market.**
eine Fleischerei.
Ī-nuh flī-sheh-RĪ.

608. —— **a pastry shop.**
eine Konditorei.
Ī-nuh kawn-dih-taw-RĪ.

609. —— **a shoemaker.**
ein Schuhmacher.
īn SHOO-mah-kher.

610. —— **a shoe store.**
ein Schuhgeschäft.
īn SHOO-geh-sheft.

611. —— **a tailor shop.**
eine Schneiderei.
Ī-nuh shnī-deh-RĪ.

612. —— **a watchmaker.**
ein Uhrmacher.
īn OOR-mah-kher.

BOOKSTORE AND STATIONER'S

SIDE FIVE, BAND 2

613. Where is there [a bookstore]?
Wo ist [ein Buchladen]?
vo ist [īn BOOKH-lah-den]?

614. —— **a stationer.**
ein Papiergeschäft.
īn pah-PEER-geh-sheft.

615. —— **a news dealer.**
ein Zeitungshändler.
īn TSĪ-toongs-hend-ler.

616. I want to buy [a book].
Ich möchte [ein Buch] kaufen.
ish MERSH-tuh [īn bookh] KOW-fen.

617. —— **a guidebook.**
ein Reisehandbuch.
īn RĪ-zuh-hahnt-bookh.

618. —— **a dictionary.**
ein Wörterbuch.
īn VERR-ter-bookh.

619. —— **a magazine.**
eine Zeitschrift.
Ī-nuh TSĪT-shrift.

620. —— **a map of Germany.**
eine Karte von Deutschland.
Ī-nuh KAHR-tuh fun DOYTSH-lahnt.

621. —— **a newspaper.**
eine Zeitung.
Ī-nuh TSĪ-toong.

622. I should like [some envelopes].
Ich möchte [Kuverts] kaufen.
ish MERSH-tuh [koo-VEHRS] KOW-fen.

623. —— **ink.**
Tinte.
TIN-tuh.

624. —— **writing paper.**
Schreibpapier.
SHRĪP-pah-peer.

625. —— **a fountain pen.**
eine Füllfeder.
Ī-nuh FEWL-fay-der.

626. —— **a pencil.**
einen Bleistift.
Ī-nen BLĪ-shtift.

627. —— **picture postcards.**
Ansichtskarten.
AHN-zishts-kahr-ten.

628. —— **wrapping paper.**
Packpapier.
PAHK-pah-peer.

629. —— **string.**
Bindfaden.
BINT-fah-den.

CIGAR STORE

630. Where is the nearest cigar store?
Wo ist der nächste Zigarrenladen?
vo ist dehr NAYK-stuh tsih-GAHR-ren-lah-den?

631. I want [some cigars].
Ich möchte [ein paar Zigarren] haben.
ish MERSH-tuh [īn pahr tsih-GAHR-ren] HAH-ben.

632. —— **a pack of American cigarettes.**
ein Päckchen amerikanische Zigaretten.
īn PEK-shen ah-may-ree-KAH-nish-uh tsih-gah-RET-ten.

633. —— **a leather cigarette case.**
ein echtledernes Zigarettenetui.
īn ES̄H̄T-lay-der-nes tsih-gah-RET-ten-AY-twee.

634. —— **a lighter.**
ein Feuerzeug.
īn FOY-er-tsoyk.

635. —— **pipe tobacco.**
Pfeifentabak.
PFĪ-fen-tah-bahk.

636. —— **Do you have a match?**
Haben Sie ein Streichholz?
HAH-ben zee īn SHTRĪKH-hohlts?

CAMERA SHOP

SIDE FIVE, BAND 3

637. **I want a roll of film for this camera.**
Ich möchte einen Film für diesen Apparat haben.
ish̄ MĒR̄S̄H̄-tuh Ī-nen film fewr DEE-zen ah-pah-RAHT HAH-ben.

638. **What is the charge for developing a roll of color film?**
Was kostet es einen Farbfilm zu entwickeln?
vahs KAW-stet es Ī-nen FAHRP-film tsoo ent-VIK-keln?

639. **When will they be ready?**
Wann werden sie fertig sein?
vahn VEHR-den zee FEHR-tish̄ zīn?

640. May I take a snapshot of you?
Dürfte ich Sie fotographieren?
DEWRF-tuh ish zee fo-toh-grah-FEE-ren?

PHARMACY

641. Where is there a pharmacy where English is spoken?
Gibt es hier eine Apotheke wo jemand Englisch spricht?
gipt es heer I-nuh ah-paw-TAY-kuh vo YAY-mahnt ENG-lish shprisht?

642. Can you fill this prescription immediately?
Können Sie dieses Rezept sofort zubereiten?
KER-nen zee DEE-zes ray-TSEPT zo-FORT TSOO-beh-ri-ten?

643. Do you have [adhesive tape]?
Haben Sie [Heftpflaster]?
HAH-ben zee [HEFT-pflah-ster]?

644. —— alcohol.
Alkohol.
AHL-ko-hohl.

645. —— antiseptic.
ein Desinfektionsmittel.
in des-in-fek-TSYAWNS-mit-tel.

646. —— aspirin.
Aspirin.
ahs-pee-REEN.

647. —— an icebag.
einen Eisbeutel.
I-nen IS-boy-tel.

648. —— **a hairbrush.**
eine Haarbürste.
Ī-nuh HAHR-bewr-stuh.

649. —— **a toothbrush.**
eine Zahnbürste.
Ī-nuh TSAHN-bewr-stuh.

650. —— **face cream.**
Gesichtskreme.
geh-ZISHTS-kray-muh.

651. —— **a comb.**
einen Kamm.
Ī-nen kahm.

652. —— **corn pads.**
Hühneraugenpflaster.
HEW-ner-ow-gen-pflah-ster.

653. —— **cotton.**
Watte.
VAHT-tuh.

654. —— **a deodorant.**
ein Geruchbefreiungsmittel.
īn geh-ROOKH-beh-frī-oongs-mit-tel.

655. —— **cleaning fluid.**
Fleckenwasser.
FLEK-ken-vahs-ser.

656. —— **iodine.**
Jod.
yoht.

657. —— **a mild laxative.**
ein mildes Abführmittel.
īn MIL-des AHP-fewr-mit-tel.

658. —— **lipstick.**
einen Lippenstift.
Ī-nen LIP-pen-shtift.

659. —— **powder.**
Puder.
POO-der.

660. —— **rouge.**
Rouge.
roozh.

661. —— **bobby pins.**
Haarnadeln.
HAHR-nah-deln.

662. —— **safety pins.**
Sicherheitsnadeln.
ZIH-sher-hīts-nah-deln.

663. —— **a razor.**
einen Rasierapparat.
Ī-nen rah-ZEER-ah-pah-raht.

664. —— **razor blades.**
Rasierklingen.
rah-ZEER-kling-en.

665. —— **sanitary napkins.**
Binden.
BIN-den.

666. —— **a sedative.**
ein Beruhigungsmittel.
īn beh-ROO-ih-goongs-mit-tel.

667. —— **shampoo.**
ein Shampoo.
īn SHAHM-poo.

668. —— **a shaving lotion.**
ein Rasierwasser.
īn rah-ZEER-vahs-ser.

669. —— **shaving cream (brushless).**
eine Rasierkreme (ohne Pinsel).
Ī-nuh rah-ZEER-kray-muh (O-nuh PIN-zel).

670. —— **sunglasses.**
Sonnenbrillen.
ZAWN-nen-bril-len.

671. —— **suntan oil.**
Sonnenöl.
ZAWN-nen-ērl.

672. —— **a thermometer.**
ein Thermometer.
īn tehr-maw-MAY-ter.

673. —— **a tube of toothpaste.**
eine Tube Zahnpasta.
Ī-nuh TOO-buh TSAHN-pahs-tah.

LAUNDRY AND DRY CLEANING

SIDE SIX, BAND 1

674. Where is [the laundry]?
Wo ist [die Wäscherei]?
vo ist [dee veh-sheh-RĪ]?

675. —— **the dry cleaner.**
die chemische Reinigungsanstalt.
dee SHAY-mih-shuh RĪ-nih-goongs-ahn-shtahlt.

676. I want these shirts [washed] mended.
Ich möchte diese Hemden [waschen lassen] flicken lassen.
ish MERSH-tuh DEE-zuh HEM-den [VAH-shen LAHS-sen] FLIK-ken LAHS-sen.

667. No starch.
Nicht stärken.
nisht SHTEHR-ken.

678. I want this suit [cleaned] pressed.
Ich möchte diesen Anzug [reinigen lassen] bügeln lassen.
ish MERSH-tuh DEE-zen AHN-tsook [RĪ-nih-gen LAHS-sen] BEW-geln LAHS-sen.

679. The belt is missing.
Der Gürtel fehlt.
dehr GEWR-tel faylt.

680. Can you sew on this button?
Können Sie diesen Knopf annähen?
KERN-nen zee DEE-zen knawpf AHN-nay-en?

681. Repair the zipper.
Reparieren Sie den Reissverschluss.
reh-pah-REE-ren zee dayn RĪS-fehr-shloos.

BARBERSHOP AND BEAUTY PARLOR

682. Where is there [a beauty parlor]?
Wo ist [ein Damen-Friseur]?
vo ist [īn DAH-men-free-zerr]?

683. —— a barbershop.
ein Herren-Friseur.
īn HEHR-ren-free-zerr.

684. A haircut, please.
Haarschneiden, bitte.
HAHR-shnī-den, BIT-tuh.

685. Not too short.*
Nicht zu kurz.
nisht tsoo koorts.

686. No lotion, please.
Kein Haarwasser, bitte.
kin HAHR-vahs-ser, BIT-tuh.

687. Please give me a shave.
Bitte rasieren Sie mich.
BIT-tuh rah-ZEE-ren zee mish.

688. Please give me a shampoo.
Bitte schampunieren Sie mich.
BIT-tuh shahm-poo-NEE-ren zee mish.

689. A hair set.
Eine Wasserwelle.
I-nuh VAHS-ser-vel-luh.

690. A permanent.
Eine Dauerwelle.
I-nuh DOW-er-vel-luh.

691. A manicure.
Eine Maniküre.
I-nuh mah-nee-KEW-ruh.

692. A facial.
Eine Gesichtsmassage.
I-nuh geh-ZISHTS-mah-sah-zhuh.

693. A massage.
Eine Kopfmassage.
I-nuh KAWPF-mah-sah-zhuh.

694. A shoeshine, please.
Die Schuhe putzen, bitte.
dee SHOO-uh POOT-sen, BIT-tuh.

* Speaker should have said "short".

HEALTH AND ILLNESS

SIDE SIX, BAND 2

695. I wish to see an American doctor.
Ich möchte einen amerikanischen Arzt aufsuchen.
ish MERSH-tuh I-nen ah-may-ree-KAH-nish-en ahrtst OWF-zoo-khen.

697. Is the doctor [at home] in his office?
Ist der Herr Doktor [zu Hause] in seinem Sprechzimmer?
ist dehr hehr DAWK-tor [tsoo HOW-zuh] in ZI-nem SHPRESH-tsim-mer?

698. I do not sleep well.
Ich schlafe nicht gut.
ish SHLAH-fuh nisht goot.

699. I have [a headache].
Ich habe [Kopfschmerzen].
ish HAH-buh [KAWPF-shmehr-tsen].

700. —— **an allergy.**
eine Allergie.
I-nuh ahl-lehr-GEE.

701. —— **a cold.**
eine Erkältung.
I-nuh ehr-KEL-toong.

702. —— **a cough.**
einen Husten.
I-nen HOO-sten.

703. —— **constipation.**
Verstopfung.
fehr-STAWP-foong.

704. —— **diarrhœa.**
Durchfall.
DOORSH-fahl.

705. —— **a fever.**
Fieber.
FEE-ber.

706. —— **a sore throat.**
Halsschmerzen.
HAHLS-shmehr-tsen.

707. I have indigestion.
Ich habe mir den Magen verdorben.
ish HAH-buh meer dayn MAH-gen fehr-DOR-ben.

708. I am nauseated.
Mir ist übel.
meer ist EW-bel.

709. Must I stay in bed?
Muss ich im Bett bleiben?
moos ish im bet BLI-ben?

710. I feel [better] worse.
Ich fühle mich [besser] schlechter.
ish FEW-luh mish [BES-ser] SHLESH-ter.

711. There is something in my eye.
Mir ist etwas ins Auge geflogen.
meer ist ET-vahs ins OW-guh geh-FLOH-gen.

712. I have a pain in my chest.
Ich habe Brustschmerzen.
ish HAH-buh BROOST-shmehr-tsen.

713. When do you think I'll be able to continue my trip?
Wann, glauben Sie, kann ich meine Reise fortsetzen?
vahn, GLOW-ben zee, kahn ish MĪ-nuh RĪ-zuh FAWRT-zet-tsen?

DENTIST

714. Do you know a good dentist?
Kennen Sie einen guten Zahnarzt?
KEN-nen zee Ī-nen GOO-ten TSAHN-ahrtst?

715. This tooth hurts.
Dieser Zahn schmerzt.
DEE-zer tsahn shmehrtst.

716. Can you fix it temporarily?
Können Sie es provisorisch in Ordnung bringen?
KERN-nen zee es pro-vee-ZOH-rish in ORD-noong BRING-en?

717. I have lost a filling.
Ich habe eine Plombe verloren.
ish HAH-buh Ī-nuh PLOHM-buh fehr-LO-ren.

718. I do not want the tooth extracted.
Ich möchte mir den Zahn nicht ziehen lassen.
ish MERSH-tuh meer dayn tsahn nisht TSEE-en LAHS-sen.

CONVERSATION AT THE POST OFFICE
(At normal rate of speech)
SIDE SIX, BAND 3

719. Ich möchte diesen Brief nach den Vereinigten Staaten schicken. Wieviel Porto kostet das?

I would like to send this letter to the United States. How much postage is that please?

720. Mit gewöhnlicher Post dreissig Pfennig, per Luftpost sechzig Pfennig.

By regular mail 30 Pfennig. By airmail 60 Pfennig.

721. Geben Sie mir bitte zwanzig Marken à 10 und fünf à 20.

Please let me have twenty 10-Pfennig stamps and five 20-Pfennig stamps.

722. Das macht insgesamt drei Mark. Der Briefkasten ist gleich hier links.

That will be three Marks all together. The mailbox is right here to the left.

723. Vielen Dank. Wo kann ich ein Paket aufgeben?

Thank you very much. Where can I mail a package?

724. Bei der Paketannahme. Nächster Schalter rechts.

At the parcel-post window. Next window to the right.

725. Was enthält Ihr Paket?

What does your parcel contain?

726. Nur ein paar Bücher und Geschenke.
Only a few books and presents.

727. Ist irgend etwas Zerbrechliches darin?
Does it contain anything breakable?

728. Nein. Kann ich das Paket versichern? Wieviel würde das kosten?
No. Can I insure the package? How much would that be?

729. Wie hoch wollen Sie es denn versichern? Es kostet fünfzig Pfennig pro fünfundzwanzig Mark Versicherung.
For how much do you want to insure it? The rate is 50 Pfennig per 25 Mark insurance.

730. Gut, bitte versichern Sie es für fünfundsiebzig Mark.
Very well, please insure it for 75 Marks.

731. Bitte füllen Sie dieses Formular aus. Das macht zusammen vier Mark neunundvierzig Pfennig; zwei neunundneunzig Porto und eine Mark fünfzig für die Versicherung.
Please fill out this form. The total charge is 4 Marks 49; 2 Marks 99 for the postage and 1 Mark 50 for the insurance.

732. Bekomme ich einen Empfangsschein?
Do I get a receipt?

733. Jawohl. Bitte unterschreiben Sie dieses Formular.
Yes. Please sign this form.

734. Gut. Recht vielen Dank.
Very well. Thank you very much.

AT THE TELEPHONE

(At normal rate of speech)

735. Zentrale? Fernamt bitte.
Operator? Long-distance, please.

736. Einen Augenblick, bitte.
One moment, please.

737. Fernamt? Ich möchte ein Ferngespräch nach Mannheim anmelden. Bitte verbinden Sie mich mit Mannheim sechs null vier zwo* sieben.
Long-distance? I would like to place a long-distance call to Mannheim. Please connect me with Mannheim 6-0427.

738. Mit Voranmeldung?
Person-to-person call?

739. Nein.
No.

740. Ihre Nummer, bitte?
Your number, please?

741. Bremerhaven neun sieben fünf acht. Und bitte unterbrechen Sie mich nach drei Minuten.
Bremerhaven 9758. And please let me know when three minutes are up.

742. Wie Sie wünschen. Ihr Teilnehmer meldet sich schon.
As you wish. Your party is answering already.

743. Hallo; hier Heinz Mahler. Könnte ich mit Herrn Gustav Leander sprechen?
Hello. This is Heinz Mahler speaking. May I speak to Mr. Gustav Leander?

* In telephoning, 2 is called "zwo" (tsvo) instead of "zwei" to avoid confusion with "drei" (three).

744. Wie, bitte? Sprechen Sie etwas lauter bitte. Die Verbindung ist nicht besonders gut.
I beg your pardon; speak a bit louder, please. The connection is not very good.

745. Hier Heinz Mahler. Ich möchte Herrn Leander sprechen.
This is Heinz Mahler. I'd like to speak to Mr. Leander.

746. Ach so. Ja, aber Herr Leander ist leider nicht zu Hause and wird voraussichtlich nicht vor halb zehn heute Abend nach Hause kommen.
Oh, I see. But Mr. Leander is unfortunately not at home and will probably not return until 9:30 this evening.

747. Hallo, hallo, Fernamt, Sie haben uns unterbrochen!
Hello, hello, long distance, you have cut us off!

748. Verzeihung. Ich stelle den Anschluss gleich wieder her.
I am sorry; I'll connect you again right away.

749. Hallo, Mannheim? Könnten Sie etwas an Herrn Leander ausrichten? Sagen Sie ihm bitte, dass Heinz Mahler angerufen hat. Ich werde Sonntag in Mannheim ankommen und im Schweizer Hof übernachten und zwar in Zimmer sechshundertvier.
Hello, Mannheim? Could you leave a message for Mr. Leander? Please tell him that Heinz Mahler called. I am arriving in Mannheim

on Sunday and will spend the night at the Hotel Switzerland. My room number will be 604.

750. Einen Augenblick, bitte. Ich möchte mir das aufschreiben. Schweizer Hof. Haben Sie Zimmer fünfhundertvier gesagt?

One moment, please. I'd like to write that down. Hotel Switzerland. Did you say Room 504?

751. Nein, Sie haben mich falsch verstanden; sechshundertvier.

No, you misunderstood me; 604.

752. Schön, alles in Ordnung.

Very good.

753. Verzeihen Sie die Störung.

I'm sorry to have bothered you.

754. Nicht im Geringsten. Ich werde Herrn Leander alles bestens ausrichten.

Not at all. I'll see to it that Mr. Leander gets the message.

755. Vielen Dank. Auf Wiedersehen.

Thanks very much. Goodbye.

756. Auf Wiedersehen.

Goodbye.

SENDING A CABLEGRAM

(At normal rate of speech)

757. Ich möchte ein Telegramm nach den Vereinigten Staaten aufgeben. Wie hoch ist die Gebühr?

I should like to send a cablegram to the United States. What is the rate?

758. **Ein gewöhnliches Telegramm kostet pro Wort dreiundneunzig Pfennig nach Neu York und eine Mark neunundzwanzig ausserhalb Neu York.**
A regular telegram is 93 Pfennigs per word to New York City and 1 Mark 29 outside New York.

759. **Was ist die Mindestgebühr?**
What is the minimum?

760. **Die Mindestgebühr beträgt nur eine Mark fünfzig.**
The minimum is only 1 Mark 50.

761. **Könnte ich stattdessen ein Brieftelegramm nach Amerika senden?**
Could I send a night letter instead to America?

762. **Jawohl, Sie können ein Brieftelegramm zu ermässigter Gebühr senden. Allerdings ist die Mindestgebühr zehn Mark dreiundzwanzig nach Neu York. Dafür können Sie zweiundzwanzig Worte schreiben.**
Yes, you can send a night letter at a lower rate. In that case, the minimum is 10 Marks 23 to New York, for which you are allowed 22 words.

763. **Wann würde das Brieftelegramm ankommen?**
When would the night letter arrive?

764. **Nicht vor morgen früh.**
Not before tomorrow morning.

765. **Und das gewöhnliche Telegramm?**
And the regular telegram?

766. Voraussichtlich binnen fünf Stunden.
Most probably within five hours.

767. Dann werde ich ein gewöhnliches Telegramm aufgeben. Könnte ich ein paar Formulare haben?
In that case I'll send a regular telegram. Could I have a couple of forms?

768. Sie liegen dort auf dem Schreibpult. Schreiben Sie bitte Ihren Namen und Ihre Adresse in Blockschrift und bringen Sie mir das ausgefüllte Formular.
There are some on the desk over there. Please print your name and address and return the filled-in form to me.

769. Vielen Dank.
Thanks very much.

TIME

SIDE SIX, BAND 4

770. What time is it?
Wieviel Uhr ist es?
VEE-feel oor ist es?

771. It is early.
Es ist früh.
es ist frew.

772. It is (too) late.
Es ist (zu) spät.
es ist (tsoo) shpayt.

773. It is two o'clock A.M. (P.M.).
Es ist zwei Uhr (vierzehn Uhr).*
es ist tsvī oor. (FEER-tsayn oor).

774. It is half-past three (*lit.* **half-hour to four**).
Es ist halb vier.
es ist hahlp feer.

775. It is a quarter-past four.
Es ist ein Viertel nach vier.
es ist īn FEER-tel nahkh feer.

776. It is a quarter to five.
Es ist ein Viertel vor fünf.
es ist īn FEER-tel for fewnf.

777. At ten minutes to six.
Um zehn Minuten vor sechs.
oom tsayn min-OO-ten for zeks.

778. At twenty minutes past seven.
Um zwanzig Minuten nach sieben.
oom TSVAHN-tsish min-OO-ten nahkh ZEE-ben.

779. Day. Tag. *tahk.*

780. Night. Nacht. *nahkht.*

781. Midnight. Mitternacht. *MIT-ter-nahkht.*

782. Today. Heute. *HOY-tuh.*

783. Tomorrow. Morgen. *MOR-gen.*

784. In the morning. Morgens. *MOR-gens.*

785. In the afternoon. Nachmittags. *NAHKH-mit-tahks.*

786. In the evening. Abends. *AH-bents.*

* The twenty-four hour system is more commonly used in Europe than in the United States. One to twelve P.M. are therefore expressed in numbers from thirteen to twenty-four.

787. Yesterday. Gestern. *GES-tern.*

788. Last night. Gestern Abend. *GES-tern AH-bent.*

789. Last month. Voriger Monat. *FOR-ih-ger mo-NAHT.*

790. Last year. Voriges Jahr. *FOR-ih-ges yahr.*

791. Next week. Nächste Woche. *NAYK-stuh VAW-khuh.*

DAYS OF THE WEEK

792. Monday. Montag. *MOHN-tahk.*

793. Tuesday. Dienstag. *DEENS-tahk.*

794. Wednesday. Mittwoch. *MIT-vawkh.*

795. Thursday. Donnerstag. *DAWN-ners-tahk.*

796. Friday. Freitag. *FRĪ-tahk.*

797. Saturday. Samstag oder Sonnabend.* *ZAHMS-tahk O-der ZAWN-ah-bent.*

798. Sunday. Sonntag. *ZAWN-tahk.*

MONTHS

799. January. Januar. *YAH-noo-ahr.*

800. February. Februar. *FAY-broo-ahr.*

801. March. März. *mehrts.*

802. April. April. *ah-PRIL.*

803. May. Mai. *mī.*

804. June. Juni. *YOO-nee.*

805. July. Juli. *YOO-lee.*

* Both forms are in common use.

806. August. August. *ow-GŎŎST.*

807. September. September. *zep-TEM-ber.*

808. October. Oktober. *awk-TOH-ber.*

809. November. November. *no-VEM-ber.*

810. December. Dezember. *day-TSEM-ber.*

SEASONS AND WEATHER

811. Spring. Frühling. *FREW-ling.*

812. Summer. Sommer. *ZAWM-mer.*

813. Autumn. Herbst. *hehrpst.*

814. Winter. Winter. *VIN-ter.*

815. It is warm. Es ist warm. *es ist vahrm.*

816. It is cold. Es ist kalt. *es ist kahlt.*

817. The weather is good. Das Wetter ist schön. *dahs VET-ter ist shērn.*

818. The weather is bad. Das Wetter ist schlecht. *dahs VET-ter ist shlesh̄t.*

819. It is raining. Es regnet. *es RAYG-net.*

NUMBERS

SIDE SIX, BAND 5

820. One. Eins. *īns.*

Two. Zwei. *tsvī.*

Three. Drei. *drī.*

Four. Vier. *feer.*

Five. Fünf. *fewnf.*

Six. Sechs. *zeks.*

Seven. Sieben. *ZEE-ben.*

Eight. Acht. *ahkht.*

Nine. Neun. *noyn.*

Ten. Zehn. *tsayn.*

Eleven. Elf. *elf.*

Twelve. Zwölf. *tsverlf.*

Thirteen. Dreizehn. *DRĪ-tsayn.*

Fourteen. Vierzehn. *FIHR-tsayn.*

Fifteen. Fünfzehn. *FEWNF-tsayn.*

Sixteen. Sechzehn. *ZESH-tsayn.*

Seventeen. Siebzehn. *ZEEP-tsayn.*

Eighteen. Achtzehn. *AHKHT-tsayn.*

Nineteen. Neunzehn. *NOYN-tsayn.*

Twenty. Zwanzig. *TSVAHN-tsish.*

Twenty-one. Einundzwanzig. *ĪN-oont-tsvahn-tsish.*

Twenty-two. Zweiundzwanzig. *TSVI-oont-tsvahn-tsish.*

Thirty. Dreissig. *DRĪ-sish.*

Forty. Vierzig. *FIHR-tsish.*

Fifty. Fünfzig. *FEWNF-tsish.*

Sixty. Sechzig. *ZESH-tsish.*

Seventy. Siebzig. *ZEEP-tsish.*

Eighty. Achtzig. *AHKHT-tsish.*

Ninety. Neunzig. *NOYN-tsish.*

One hundred. Einhundert. *ĪN-hoon-dert.*

Two hundred. Zweihundert. *TSVĪ-hoon-dert.*

One thousand. Eintausend. *ĪN-tow-zent.*

Two thousand. Zweitausend. *TSVĪ-tow-zent.*

One million. Eine Million. *Ī-nuh meel-YOHN.*

SIGNS AND PUBLIC NOTICES

(The following list of signs and notices is not recorded. For your convenience, these lists have been alphabetized according to the German language.)

This list includes most of the recurring signs and notices that one sees on the streets and public places of a city. There is no need to memorize this list now, but do review it when you arrive in the country. If you plan to drive, the study of road signs is, of course, imperative. With the help of this list or a pocket dictionary, make an effort to learn the meaning of common signs you see. It is an excellent way to build your vocabulary in the course of your travels, because signs and notices, by and large, reflect the current language that answers everyday practical needs. You will also find that when you understand almost all the common signs you see around you, you will be more at home and confident in your new environment.

PUBLIC NOTICES

821. Abfahrt. Departure.
822. Abfallkasten. Rubbish bin.
823. Abort. Toilet.
824. Absender. Sender.
825. Ankunft. Arrival.
826. Aufzug. Elevator.
827. Augenarzt. Oculist.
828. Ausgang. Exit.
829. Auskunft. Information.
830. Ausschank. Buffet; refreshments.
831. Autoreparatur. Auto repairs.
832. Autovermietung. Autos for hire.

833. Bäckerei. Bakery.
834. Baden verboten! Bathing prohibited.
835. Bahnsteigkarte. Platform ticket.
836. Bank. Bank.
837. Bar. Bar.
838. Baustelle. Men at work.
839. Bedienung. Service.
840. Bekanntmachung. Public notice.
841. Belegt. No vacancy.
842. Besetzt. Occupied.
843. Betreten verboten! Keep off.
844. Bibliothek. Library.
845. Bier. Beer.
846. Bitte die Tiere nicht füttern! Do not feed the animals.
847. Bitte läuten! Please ring.
848. Bitte Ruhe. Quiet please.
849. Bitte spülen. Please flush.
850. Blumenladen. Flower shop.
851. Börsenmakler. Stockbroker.
852. Botanischer Garten. Botanical garden.
853. Briefkasten. Mailbox.
854. Briefmarken. Stamps.
855. Buchladen. Bookshop.
856. Büffet. Buffet.

857. Chemische Reinigung. Dry cleaning.

858. Damen. Ladies.
859. Damenfriseur. Beauty parlor.
860 Damenkonfektion. Ladies' clothing.
861. Datum. Date.
862. DER. Deutsches Reisebüro. (Official German tourist agency.)
863. Dolmetscher. Interpreter.
864. Drücken. Push.

865. Eilzug. Express train.
866. Einfamilienhaus. One-family house; villa.
867. Eingang. Entrance.
868. Eingang nur für Angestellte. Employees only.
869. Eintritt (frei). Admission (free).
870. Einwurf: 10 Pfennig. Deposit 10 pfennigs.
871. Einzelhandel. Retail.
872. Eis. Ice, ices.
873. Eisdiele (*or* **Eissalon**). Ice cream parlor.
874. Elektrische Geräte. Electrical appliances.
875. Empfänger. Addressee.
876. En gros. Wholesale.
877. Erfrischung. Refreshments.
878. Expressgut. Railway express.

879. Fabrik. Factory.
880. Fahrplan. Timetable.
881. Fernruf (Anruf) für. Long-distance (telephone) call for.
882. Fernsehapparate. Television sets.
883. Feuergefahr. Danger of fire.
884. Feuermelder. Fire alarm box.
885. Fleischer. Butcher.
886. Fotograph. Photographer.
887. Fremdenzimmer. Guest rooms.
888. Friedhof. Cemetery.
889. Frisch gestrichen! Wet paint.
890. Friseur. Barbershop.

891. Garderobe. Checkroom.
892. Gebühr. Charge.
893. Gefahr. Danger.
894. Gefrorenes. Ices.
895. Geldwechsel. Money exchanged.
896. Gelegenheitskäufe. Bargains.
897. Geöffnet von . . . bis . . . Open from . . . to . . .
898. Gepäckschein. Baggage check.
899. Gepäckversicherung. Baggage insurance.
900. Geschenke. Gifts.
901. Geschlossen von . . . bis . . . Closed from . . . to . . .
902. Getränkesteuer. Liquor tax.
903. Gift! Nicht einnehmen! Poison! Not for internal use.
904. Gleis. Railroad track.
905. GmbH. Incorporated.
906. Gottesdienst. Church service.
907. Gültigkeit bis . . . Good until . . .

908. Hauptbahnhof. Main railroad station.
909. Haus- und Küchengeräte. Household ware.
910. Heiss. Hot.
911. Heizungszuschlag. Heating fee.
912. Herein! Walk in.
913. Herren. Gentlemen.

914. **Herrenfriseur.** Barbershop.
915. **Herrenkonfektion.** Men's clothing.
916. **Heute Betriebsruhe.** Closed for the day.
917. **Heute geschlossen.** Closed today.
918. **Heute Tanz.** Dancing today.
919. **Hinauf.** Up.
920. **Hinunter.** Down.
921. **Holz.** Lumber.

922. **Kaffeehaus.** Coffee house.
923. **Kalt.** Cold.
924. **Kartenausgabe.** Ticket window.
925. **Kegelbahn.** Bowling.
926. **Kein Trinkwasser.** Not for drinking purposes.
927. **Keine Vorstellung.** No performance.
928. **Kein Zutritt.** No entrance; no trespassing.
929. **Kiosk.** Newsstand.
930. **Kino.** Movie.
931. **Klingel.** Bell.
932. **Kolonialwarengeschäft.** Grocery.
933. **Konditorei.** Coffee house and Pastry shop.
934. **Krankenhaus.** Hospital.
935. **Kunsthalle.** Art gallery.
936. **Kurort.** Health resort.
937. **Kurtaxe.** Residence tax (in a health resort).

938. **Lebensmittelgeschäft.** Grocery.
939. **Leihbücherei.** Lending library.
940. **Links.** Left.
941. **Luftpost.** Airmail.

942. **Metzger.** Butcher.
943. **Mittagessen.** Lunch.
944. **Mittel zur Schönheitspflege.** Cosmetics.
945. **Möbel.** Furniture.
946. **Möblierte Zimmer zu vermieten.** Furnished rooms to let.

947. **Nähmaschine.** Sewing machine.
948. **Notbremse.** Emergency brake.

949. **Obstladen.** Fruit store.
950. **O-Bus Haltestelle.** Bus stop.
951. **Öffentlicher Fernsprecher.** Public telephone.
952. **Optiker.** Occulist.
953. **Ortsgespräch.** Local telephone call.

954. **Polizei.** Police.
955. **Postamt.** Post office.
956. **Postanweisung.** Money order.

957. **Quittung.** Receipt.

958. Rathaus. City hall.
959. Raucher. Smoking car.
960. Rauchen verboten. No smoking.
961. Rechts. Right.
962. Rechtsanwalt. Lawyer.
963. Reisebüro. Travel agency.
964. Reserviert. Reserved.

965. Schneider. Tailor; dressmaker.
966. Schnellküche. Snack bar.
967. Schnellzug. Express train.
968. Schuhputzer. Shoeshine stand.
969. Schwimmen verboten. No swimming.
970. Selbstbedienung. Self-service.
971. Sie werden gebeten . . . You are requested . . .
972. Sonn- und Feiertags geschlossen. Closed on Sundays and holidays.
973. Speisewagen. Dining car.
974. Speisezimmer. Dining room.
975. Spirituosen. Wines and liquors.
976. Sportartikel. Sports goods.
977. Spucken verboten. No spitting.
978. Stufe. Step.

979. Tiergarten. Zoo.
980. Tiergeschäft. Pet shop.
981. Toilette. Toilet.
982. Treppen. Stairs.
983. Trinkgeld. Tip.

984. Unterschrift. Signature.

985. (Hat) Verspätung. (Is) late.
986. Voll besetzt. Fully occupied.
987. Vor dem Hund wird gewarnt. Beware of the dog.
988. Vorsicht. Caution; look out.
989. Vorsicht beim aussteigen. Watch your step getting off.
990. Vorsicht Hund. Beware of the dog.
991. Vorstellung um . . . Performance at . . .

992. W.C. Toilet.
993. Weinhandlung. Wines and liquors.
994. Warteraum (*or* **Wartesaal**). Waiting room.
995. Wäscherei. Laundry.
996. Wechselstube. Money change booth.

997. Zahnarzt. Dentist.
998. Zeitungshändler. News dealer.
999. Ziehen. Pull.

1000. Zigarrenladen. Cigar store.
1001. Zoologischer Garten. Zoo.
1002. Zu den [Schiffen] Zügen. To the [boats] trains.
1003. Zu verkaufen. For sale.
1004. Zu vermieten. For rent; for hire.
1005. Zuschlag. Special fee.

ROAD SIGNS

1006. Abblenden. Dim lights.
1007. Abzweigung. Turn-off.
1008. Achtung! Attention! Caution!
1009. Anhänger. Trailer.
1010. Auf eigene Gefahr. At your own risk.
1011. Ausfahrt. Exit.
1012. Ausgenommen. Except.
1013. Auto. Automobile.
1014. Autofähre. Car ferry.

1015. Bahnübergang (un-)beschrankt. Railroad crossing (un-)gated.
1016. Baustelle. Work in progress.
1017. Bezirk. District.
1018. Brücke. Bridge.

1019. Dorf. Village.
1020. Droschkenplatz. Taxi stand.

1021. Einbahnstrasse. One-way street.
1022. Einbieger. Turn-off.
1023. Einfahrt. Entry.
1024. Ende. End of road.
1025. Enge Strasse. Narrow road.

1026. Fahrbahn. Traffic lane.
1027. Fahrbahnwechsel. Change of lane.
1028. Fahrzeug. Vehicle.
1029. Fernverkehr(-strasse). Bypass (road).
1030. Flugplatz. Airport.
1031. Freie Fahrt. Resume speed.
1032. Fussgänger. Pedestrians.
1033. Fussweg. Footpath; pedestrians.

1034. Gefahr. Danger.
1035. Gefährliche Einmündung. Dangerous junction.
1036. Gefährliche Kurve. Dangerous curve.
1037. 10% Gefälle. 10% grade.
1038. Gegenverkehr. Two-way traffic.
1039. Gegenverkehr hat Vorfahrt. Oncoming traffic has right of way.

1040. Geradeaus. Straight ahead.
1041. Gesperrt. Closed.
1042. Gewicht. Weight.
1043. Glatteis. Icy.
1044. Grenze. Border.

1045. Halt. Stop.
1046. Hauptverkehrsstrasse. Main road.
1047. Hilfsposten. First-aid station.
1048. Hochspannung. High-tension.
1049. Höchstgeschwindigkeit. Speed limit.
1050. Höhe ü.d.M. (**über dem Meer**). Altitude above sea level.

1051. Jetzt umschalten Shift now.

1052. Kehre. Hairpin curve.
1053. Keine Durchfahrt. No thoroughfare; dead end.
1054. Krad. Motorcycle.
1055. Kraftfahrzeug. Vehicle.
1056. Kraftrad. Motorcycle.
1057. Kraftwagen. Automobile.
1058. Krankenhaus. Hospital.
1059. Kreisverkehr. Traffic circle.
1060. Kreuzung. Crossroads; intersection.
1061. Kurgebiet. Quiet zone (in health resort).
1062. Kurve. Curve.
1063. Kurvenreiche Strecke. Winding road.

1064. Landkreis. County.
1065. Langsam fahren. Drive slowly.
1066. Lastwagen. Truck.
1067. Lebensgefahr. Danger of death
1068. Links fahren. Keep left.
1069. Links halten. Drive to left of this sign.

1070. Mautgebühr. Toll.
1071. Moped. Bicycle with auxiliary motor.
1072. Motorrad. Motorcycle.

1073. Nach. To (a destination).
1074. Nebenstrasse. Secondary road.
1075. Nicht [rechts] links einbiegen. No [right] left turn.
1076. Nicht überholen. No passing.

1077. Parken verboten, *or* **Parkverbot.** No parking.
1078. Parkplatz. Parking allowed.
1079. Pkw (**Personenkraftwagen**). Passenger car.
1080. Privateigentum. Private property.
1081. Privatweg. Private road.

1082. Querrinne. Dip.

1083. **Radfahrweg,** *or* **Radweg.** Cycle path.
1084. **Radweg kreutzt.** Bicycle crossing.
1085. **Rechts fahren.** Keep right.
1086. **Rechts halten.** Drive to right of this sign.
1087. **Reitpfad.** Bridle path.

1088. **Scharf.** Sharp.
1089. **Schlechte Wegstrecke (auf 2 Km).** Bad road (for 2 kilometers).
1090. **Schleudergefahr.** Slippery.
1091. **Schule.** School.
1092. **S-Kurve.** Double curve.
1093. **Sonn- und Feiertags für . . . gesperrt.** Closed on Sunday and holidays to . . .
1094. **Stadtkreis.** City district.
1095. **Steigung.** Grade.
1096. **Steil.** Steep.
1097. **Steinschlag.** Falling rocks.
1098. **Strassenarbeiten.** Road repairs.
1099. **Strassenbahn.** Tramway.
1100. **Strassennummer.** Road number.

1101. **Tankstelle.** Gas station.

1102. **Über.** Via.
1103. **Überholen verboten.** No passing.
1104. **Umleitung (über . . .).** Detour (through . . .).
1105. **Umschalten.** Shift gear.
1106. **Unterführung.** Underpass.

1107. **Verengte Fahrbahn.** Road narrows.
1108. **Verkehrsampel auf . . . Meter.** Traffic light . . . meters ahead.
1109. **Vorfahrt achten.** Give right of way.
1110. **Vorfahrtsrecht.** Right of way.
1111. **Vorsicht.** Caution.
1112. **Vorsichtig fahren.** Drive carefully.

1113. **Wildwechsel.** Deer crossing.

1114. **Zeltplatz.** Camping site.
1115. **Zoll.** Customs.
1116. **Zugbrücke.** Drawbridge.

INDEX

All the sentences, phrases, and words in this book are numbered consecutively from 1 to 1116. The entries in the Index refer to these numbers. In addition, each major section (capitalized) is indexed according to page number.